John D. Vi

FETCH MORE DOLLARS FOR YOUR DOG TRAINING BUSINESS

Dogwise Publishing
Wenatchee, Washington U.S.A.

Fetch More Dollars For Your Dog Training Business
John D. Visconti, CPDT-KA

Dogwise Publishing
A Division of Direct Book Service, Inc.
403 South Mission Street, Wenatchee, Washington 98801
1-509-663-9115, 1-800-776-2665
www.dogwisepublishing.com / info@dogwisepublishing.com

Editor in chief: Larry Woodward
Illustrations: Tim Kirby
Graphic design: Lindsay Peternell
Cover design: Jesus Cordero

Library of Congress Cataloging-in-Publication Data

Visconti, John D.
Fetch more dollars / by John D. Visconti, CPDT-KA.
pages cm
Includes bibliographical references and index.
ISBN 978-1-61781-159-3
1. Dogs--Training--Economic aspects. 2. Selling. I. Title.
SF431V57 2015
636.7'0835--dc23

2014049504

ISBN: 978-1-61781-159-3

Printed in the U.S.A.

Dedication

This book is dedicated to: my dog Pepper—without her unyielding support I undoubtedly would have completed it much sooner; those who encouraged me to write it but will likely watch Seinfeld reruns rather than read it; definitely not the guy who stole my Mother's Day flowers from my car in 1977; Paul McCartney, who by mentioning him, I figure this is my best shot at having him contact me. Every force-free trainer who has invested in themselves by purchasing this book with the goal of enriching the lives of more dogs and their owners. And my five year old goddaughter, Allie, who reminds me of the promise held in each new day.

Table of Contents

Acknowledgments

Dr. Ian Dunbar who, notwithstanding our jokes about color blindness, never turns a blind eye (or deaf ear) when I reach out for support or friendship.

Mira Leibstein, my most cherished mentor who years ago continually inspired and challenged me in ways that built my confidence rather than shaking it.

Amanda Fried who, like a parent helping a child learn to ride a bicycle, kept me from continually falling over by running alongside me when I first started writing this book.

Adrienne Hovey, who magically turned 4000 word rambles into comprehensible paragraphs. After our last edit she was heard muttering, "I can't take this &%$$^# anymore" while boarding a boat headed for the Galapagos Islands, never to be seen or heard from again.

April Henry, who provided me with a boost when my creative rudder got stuck in the mud.

The entire staff at Dogwise (particularly my second editor, Larry Woodward, last seen wearing a "Galapagos Islands or Bust" t-shirt) who, in guiding me through my maiden publishing voyage, have been incredibly supportive and respectful of my manner of expressing myself and who went out on a limb to publish a book about a subject that potentially holds as much interest as a book entitled "The Expurgated History of Brussels Sprouts."

Trainers and friends (alphabetically listed): Mary Jean Alsina, Malena Demartini-Price, Jennifer Shryock, Anne Springer, Heidi Steinbeck, Matt Tuzzo, and former APDT president Michelle Douglas who represent everything that is good about our field and have been wonderfully supportive of me.

A German Shepherd named Jasmine who helped me discover my love for training.

And of course, my dog Pepper, who has sharpened my sales skills by constantly inspiring me to devise new ways to persuade her.

Welcome to Force-Free Selling

As the old adage goes, if you want milk from a cow, sitting on a stool in the middle of a field waiting for a cow to back up to you is probably not a sound strategy. Similarly, hoping your dog training website or other social media will generate tons of sales, without some help from you, does not bode well for the future of your business. "If you build it, they will come" might be a great concept for a movie, but in the field of dog training, it's a precursor to saying "I used to have a training business, but now I just do it as a hobby."

If you are like me and so many other trainers, you entered this field to help owners and their dogs to live better lives. The idea of acting as a salesperson for your dog training business may make you very uncomfortable, especially if you associate the sales process with negative experiences you might have had with pushy telemarketers or when buying a car from a dealership. And even though the sales process is critical to the health of any training business, and in turn the life quality of dogs and their owners, trainers often avoid it like the proverbial plague. Many trainers feel about selling as Woody Allen noted about death, "I'm not afraid of death. I just don't want to be there when it happens."

What you may not know is that it's likely you're already on your way to becoming an effective salesperson. You probably already possess many of the traits of highly effective salespeople and you're already *utilizing* them on a daily basis with some excellent results. It's simply a matter of refocusing and redirecting those skills in order to help more dog owners by gaining them as clients.

The better news is that you are a goal-driven and highly motivated individual. The fact that you are a professional dog trainer, coupled with your purchase of this book, speaks volumes about your motivation and desire for improvement. The road to self-improvement is no different than in dog training—you need motivation to learn new behaviors. The way I figure, the only thing standing between us and greatness is, well, us. If you'd like to change what trainers often consider to be the most distasteful part of their job—selling—into a positive activity, this book will help you to achieve that goal.

The methodology in this book is sleaze-free. The sales approaches I discuss here are not based in gimmicks and being slick, but instead are founded on the simple concept of helping people to hire the best trainer they can: you! The methods discussed in this book have their foundations in the science of human persuasion and behavior. Just as there's no such thing as dog "whispering" there are no "sales whisperers." An effective trainer needs to possess a solid understanding of canine behavior. An effective salesperson needs to possess a solid understanding of human behavior. Dog training and selling are both learned disciplines.

While this book is written about sales, the goal is not to inspire you to think like a salesperson but rather, to think like a client. Instead of wondering, "What do I need to do in order to gain this sale?" the more effective question is "What can I do to *help* this person?" The only way you'll be able to answer that question is to think like your prospective clients. When you do, your training business will thrive.

This book will help to reduce one of the biggest obstacles to effective selling—sales anxiety. Like anything else, understanding how to channel and control anxiety (which in small amounts is a good thing) actually helps to reduce it. Here's the big secret: Even the most successful salesperson experiences anxiety when selling. When you learn how to channel that anxiety, your business will flourish and you'll be able to help more owners and their dogs.

Hopefully this book will challenge your comfort zones because learning often occurs within a context of discomfort. According to Swiss developmental psychologist Jean Piaget, two processes—assimilation and accommodation—are foundational elements of learning. Assimilation occurs when we encounter new or unfamiliar information and refer to previous experiences or knowledge in order to process it. In other words, when we assimilate, we put new information into an already existing mental file folder. On the other hand, accommodation is the process of taking new information and fitting it into our existing schema. Accommodation takes place when we either alter an existing mental file folder or create a new one to house the new experience. When assimilation and accommodation are not in balance, people enter a state of disequilibrium. This causes discomfort, which is the reason many people reject new ideas. It's easier for us to feel comfortable within an existing belief structure than to have to scrap or alter our old system and cause ourselves discomfort when doing so. If you feel discomfort while reading this book, that's great. It means you are learning and you are challenging your belief systems

Congratulations for your commitment to yourself. Your drive for self-improvement has placed you (and your clients) on the road to a less stressful, more fulfilling life. I hope you're as excited about the journey on which you're about to embark as I am.

1

What is Selling?

What is selling?

- Selling is an act in completion of a commercial activity.
- Selling is offering to exchange an item of value for a different item.
- To give or hand over (something) in exchange for money.
- The last step in the chain of commerce where a buyer exchanges cash for a seller's goods or service, or the activity of trying to bring this about.

These are just a few definitions I found for the term *selling*. It's a good thing I was unaware of these descriptions when I was first considering a career as a salesperson or I never would have become one. As dry as these are, at least they're more generous than the definition most people attribute to the activity: *Selling is what you say you do for a living if you don't want people to congregate around you at a social function*!

Let's take a more in-depth look at this age old discipline called selling. A traditional definition of selling is a process in which a product or service provided by one party (a business or an individual) is exchanged for money by another party (the client). The role of the salesperson is usually perceived as one in which he or she tries to convince the client to make such a purchase. An effective salesperson uses a variety of techniques to "close a sale." The selling process is often considered to be distasteful if you adopt the point of view that selling is something you do *to* another person. Especially if there is little or no regard as to whether or not the client really needs or will benefit from the product or service. Unfortunately this happens all too often and is why so many people shy away from selling.

Rather than thinking of selling this way, let's redefine it as something you *do to help* another person. Rather than wondering: "What do I need to do in order to gain this sale?" the more effective question is: "What can I do to help this person?" The only way you'll be able to answer that question is to think like your prospective client. The goal is not to inspire you to think like a salesperson but instead to think like a client in order to identify his or her needs.

Once you understand that selling isn't an event, but rather a mindset geared toward providing a better life for dog owners and their dogs that is interwoven into the *entire* dog training process, the more enjoyable and effective your efforts will be and the less you'll feel like you're selling. After all, you are in the business of helping people and dogs. When you do, your training business will thrive. And better still, if you perform your sales activities with a noble goal in mind, you'll never have to worry about someone asking you, "Are you now or have you ever been a salesperson?"

What are you selling? Benefits!

Successful salespeople distinguish between the tool and the product the customer is looking to purchase. Harvard marketing professor Theodore Levitt used to advise his students, "People don't want to buy a quarter-inch drill. They want a quarter-inch hole." Sell the hole, not the drill. Similarly, your clients aren't purchasing dog training. Dog training is a tool. The client purchases what that tool can *do for them*.

For example, a client might ask you to help teach her dog not to jump on guests. Your job is to reduce jumping by differentially reinforcing an incompatible behavior, perhaps sitting. But is that what your client is purchasing? No. Your client is purchasing a benefit, in this case, embarrassment reduction because jumping dogs cause much discomfiture in their owners. Your client is purchasing the benefit of increased safety because Fido jumping up and launching Grandma through the screen door and into the azalea bushes can be a safety hazard. Your client is purchasing increased control, lower levels of frustration, and stress reduction.

With that said, don't assume your clients have a complete awareness of what they're purchasing—often, you'll need to identify or clarify that for them. For example, when teaching a dog to sit while greeting guests, it's important that you spell out all the benefits of the new behavior (safe greeting for guests, impulse control, sit as a default position, context as cue, etc.) and also paint the picture of what the terminal behavior will look like as guests enter their home and are greeted by a calm, seated dog. And of course, point out the emotional benefits for all involved. Remember, people don't purchase seeds. They purchase the experience of joy when looking at flowers. When you embrace and incorporate this perspective into your sales activities, you'll have a more motivated prospect, and motivation is what we're always looking to achieve.

When you think of selling as a process in which you communicate how your skills as a dog trainer can be utilized to provide benefits to owners and their dogs, your level of discomfort about "selling" will likely decrease. But I'm sure you're not convinced yet, so read on!

2

You Already Have What it Takes to Be an Effective Salesperson

A predominant stereotype embraced by many people identifies successful salespeople as being extroverted, highly energetic, outgoing individuals; conversely, introverts are seen as standing little chance to succeed in the field of sales. You might also embrace the idea that many dog trainers are introverts, preferring the company of dogs to people. Well let's see if the myth of extroverts being the best salespeople can be exploded!

A 2013 study conducted by Adam Grant of the Wharton School of the University of Pennsylvania debunks the aforementioned stereotypical myths (Grant, 2013). In fact, the Grant study (and others as well) demonstrated *that extroverts and introverts perform at almost the same level of ineffectiveness.* In a nutshell, the study indicated that extroverts are likely to turn clients off with the excesses of their personalities. Additionally, extroverts tend to be poor listeners; consequently, they don't learn about the needs of the client. Finally, extroverts are inclined to be self-focused and don't ask enough questions when interacting with clients. Always remember, as a salesperson what you say is never as important as what you ask. Extroverts spend too much time *saying* and not enough time *asking*.

On the other hand, as expected, introverts often experience difficulties with the sales process because they don't engage the client, and they frequently don't feel comfortable enough to ask questions and do what is necessary to unearth the client's problems and goals.

So, which group *does* tend to be most successful in sales? Ambiverts.

Ambiverts are defined as those who possess traits that cover both sides of the personality range. They can be assertive when necessary, enthusiastic, and capable of persuading, while still being attentive listeners and not appearing to be arrogant or overconfident. And here's the good news: The vast majority of people are ambiverts. Chances are you are too. And customers love to purchase products from people who are similar to them.

If you'd like to see where you fall on the extrovert/ambivert/introvert scale, take this test at http://www.danpink.com/assessment/. Many people are surprised to discover that they are ambiverts. If you have believed that you can't sell because you're an introvert, you'll be in for a pleasant surprise to learn that in fact, you're likely an ambivert.

Note to extroverts and introverts: As pointed out earlier, effective selling is an acquired skill. Take heart in knowing that regardless of where you fall on the scale, you can learn to be a good salesperson. Often, extroverts don't spend the time learning their trade because they assume they will succeed by force of personality. Introverts often don't bother to study the elements of successful selling because they assume they won't succeed. In both cases, applying time and effort to developing sales skills will pay off handsomely in the end.

The top five traits of successful salespeople: news flash, you not only possess them, but you're already utilizing them

Steve W. Martin, sales strategy teacher at the USC Marshall School of Business and author of the book *Heavy Hitter Sales Linguistics: 101 Advanced Sales Call Strategies for Senior Sales-*

people, conducted an in-depth study to identify the traits of top performing salespeople. His findings were published by the *Harvard Business Review* (Martin, 2011).

What follows is a listing of some of the key personality attributes of top salespeople.

- **Modesty**: 91% of top salespeople had medium to high levels of modesty
- **Conscientiousness**: 85% of top salespeople scored high in levels of conscientiousness.
- **Achievement orientation**: 84% of the top performers tested scored very high in achievement orientation.
- **Lack of discouragement**: Less than 10% of top salespeople were classified as having high levels of discouragement.
- **Lack of gregariousness**: Overall, top performers averaged 30% lower gregariousness than below average performers. Gregariousness was defined as the "preference for being with people."

Notice the list has none of the traits typically associated with successful salespeople: extroversion, charm, slickness, etc. In fact, it's a list of some fairly mundane traits.

Shared traits of effective salespeople *and* good dog trainers

A parallel exists between the skill set of top performing sales reps and dog trainers. If you're actively training, you not only possess the above skills, but you're regularly utilizing them. Need proof?

- **Modesty**. When you are training, are you boastful? Do you make yourself the center of attention? Are you pushy or egotistical?
- **Conscientiousness**. Are you "winging it" during your training sessions, or do you have a plan? Are you reliable? Do you show up on time? Do you feel a sense of responsibility to your clients?

- **Achievement orientation**. When you train, are you focused on your goals? Do you have a terminal behavior in mind when training a dog? Are you are measuring progress toward your goals and adjusting accordingly during the training process?
- **Lack of discouragement.** When a dog doesn't respond, do you give up? When the owner's mechanics need work, do you help, or simply quit on him or her? Do you utilize splits and changes in criteria to achieve your training goals?
- **Lack of gregariousness**. One simple question: Do you often prefer hanging out with the dog, rather than the owners?

Another trait that provides dog trainers with the potential to be very effective salespeople is something called modeling. Modeling is our brain's capacity to link similar experiences and similar data into predictable patterns. As a dog trainer, you're constantly engaged in modeling through your observation of the dog's responses to stimuli. From the information that you gain through modeling you are able to establish criteria, splits, etc. while training. As trainers we are often able to predict a dog's behavior before it happens. This often surprises our clients but essentially we're simply engaged in modeling.

Similarly, effective salespeople learn through the same process of gathering and sorting information obtained through sales calls and client interaction. From this foundation, salespeople can predict what will occur and what they need to do, either proactively or in response to a client's communication, in order to achieve a positive outcome.

Just as you are able to pick up on the slightest nuances in a dog's body language and behavior, successful salespeople possess an ability to store and retrieve verbal, nonverbal, factual, and intuitive information gained through sales calls. This results in a greater likelihood to win business because they are able to learn from their past mistakes and not repeat them.

As trainers we all learn through modeling. To not do so would doom us to repeatedly making the same mistakes which would negatively impact our training outcomes and even place us in harm's way at times.

If we define selling as persuading, you are already utilizing sales skills during your training sessions. Need more convincing?

- While training, you are persuading the dog that if he responds as coached, good things will happen.
- You are convincing the owners that their dog has the capability to learn.
- You are encouraging the owners to recognize that they have the capability to teach.
- You are convincing everyone in the room that you're the person who can make it all come together.

You'll notice the many similarities between the skill sets required to be effective in the disciplines of dog training and selling. I believe that good dog trainers have the potential to be *extremely* effective salespeople because of these shared skill sets. It's simply a matter of redirecting and refining those skills to achieve a different terminal behavior—the conversion of a prospect into a satisfied client.

3

Good Salespeople Are Made, Not Born

During my years in sales and sales consulting, I have discovered that many people believe the success of effective salespeople is directly related to natural, native abilities, rather than learned skills. Holding this belief is no different than the beliefs of your client who comments, "You have a *way* with dogs." Or, "You make it look so easy." Yes, you appear to be a *natural* but your ability to achieve a positive training outcome is directly related to the many hours you spent studying and practicing to become an effective trainer. Regardless of the affinity you have for training and whatever native abilities you may possess, without a formal education your chances of becoming an effective trainer are slim. The same applies to salespeople. My beginning in sales is a testament to this fact.

My experience in the world of sales

In 1991, prepared to set the sales world ablaze, I accepted a sales position with a commercial printing company. Yes indeed, I believed that a Natural Salesperson had been born. However my earnings were not what I had envisioned. My earnings were such that in order to pay my bills I had to sell my Gibson 160E John Lennon acoustic guitar. My red Nissan 240Z was driven off by someone who left me with a bank check and a melancholy heart. I sold my Movado watch and also completely drained my savings. I'm sure some of my less important internal organs would have been up for sale if I had remained on the same unproductive path. At my lowest point, for the good of the company, I was politely asked by the human resources manager if I would mind being injected with malaria. Eventually, we settled on me resigning my position. It was a great wake up call. Long story short, I learned that the discipline of selling is no different than any other acquired skill. Effort = results.

After that experience, I applied myself to learning my craft, I began to experience different results. And thankfully, I still own all of my original internal organs. Over the next 23 years, I sold in excess of $36 million of commercial printing. Those sales were compiled over 13,548 individual transactions. My sales were easily more than double the measure of even the most successful salespeople in my industry. What I learned is that you don't need to be a "natural" in order to succeed, but it does require dedication and effort. Take heart in the fact that just as there are no natural doctors, attorneys, and dog trainers, there are no natural salespeople. At most, there are people who have innate skill sets that help them perform certain jobs with more ease than those who need to learn their trade. But you *can* learn to become an effective salesperson—I did. While some salespeople have inborn skills that help them to succeed, after having coached and managed over 200 salespeople in my career, I am confident that with dedication and effort, *anyone* can improve their sales skills.

Becoming a good salesperson

My research and experience has taught me that following these few simple rules can lead to success in selling:

1. Remember to sell what your client is looking to purchase.
2. You are selling all the time even if you don't know it.
3. You will need to overcome self-doubts and misconceptions.

4. Remember, you can choose *not to be* "that kind" of a salesperson.
5. If you help your clients succeed with their dogs, good things will follow.

Let's review these rules in some detail.

Remember to sell what your client is looking to purchase

Many years ago, IBM's sales slogan was based on the value that what they were selling was a good night's sleep. IBM knew it wasn't in the hardware business—it was in the *reliability* business. Essentially, IBM was saying, "Buy our product and sleep well, knowing that while you're sleeping, our hardware isn't." IBM was selling a benefit called *peace of mind.*

When inventor Marion A. Trozzolo introduced his new Teflon coated "Happy Pan," he didn't sell his creation by asking: "How'd ya like to buy some Teflon coated pans?" Instead, he trumpeted the benefits of "An amazing new concept in cooking. Nothing sticks to the Happy Pan." Heck, this new concept was so amazing even the pan was happy! Trozzolo sold happiness, not Teflon.

What you are selling when you offer dog training services to a client is not dog training per se, but rather the benefits of a well-trained dog as mentioned in Chapter 1. We'll get into an in-depth discussion about benefits later in this book, but it's important to point out that dozens of neuroscience based studies have demonstrated that people are powerfully driven to purchase products and services based on emotions and perceived benefits. In fact, there's a term to describe the connection between neurochemistry (the combined functions of the nervous system and brain) and buyer behavior—it's called "*buyology*." Remember, people don't purchase obedience training from you. They purchase the emotional benefits of peace of mind, stress reduction and improved quality of life through having a well-trained dog. When you highlight the emotional benefits provided by your services, your potential client is much more likely to hire you.

The Big Secret—you are selling all day long even if you don't know it

If we define sales as the freedictionary.com does, "To persuade [another] to recognize the worth or desirability of something," the process of selling is an activity in which we engage every day. We sell our rules to our kids. We sell our ideas to spouses/significant others. We sell the value of desired behaviors to our client's dogs. Have you ever engaged in a Facebook debate about dog training methodology? Guess what? You're selling. You are attempting to persuade another human being to embrace your point of view. Have you ever engaged in motivating a dog to come to you on a recall and then paid handsomely for compliance? Once again, you're selling.

In his book, *To Sell Is Human: The Surprising Truth About Moving Others*, Daniel Pink refers to these activities and hundreds of others, as "Non-Sales Selling." Pink states "I discovered that I spend a sizeable portion of [my days] selling in a broader sense—persuading, influencing, and convincing others." Pink estimates that we spend 40% of our days "selling" (Pink, 2012).

It's extremely important to embrace the fact that we engage in selling very often during the course of our days. Doing so will help to normalize the activity and reduce your likelihood to engage in sales avoidance behaviors. As noted by Robert Louis Stevenson, "Everyone lives by selling something."

Overcoming self-doubts and misconceptions

Without first removing sales avoidance defense mechanisms, your business will never have the chance to grow to its fullest potential and, as a consequence, fewer dogs will benefit from your training skills. That many trainers feel they can't sell is a fallacy which they have quite effectively and unfortunately sold to themselves.

I have encountered many dog trainers who, in order to avoid sales anxiety, have built a negative conditioned emotional response (–CER) toward the sales process. The thought process and subsequent behavior progression for building this barrier goes something like this:

I just can't do it! In fact, you've already undertaken a much more difficult task when you decided to become a dog trainer. Having done both, I found it more difficult to acquire dog training skills than sales skills. Since the foundation for sales is the knowledge of human behavior and motivation, our experience as human beings gives us a head start when learning about sales. On the other hand, I still can't figure out why my dog Pepper does some of what she does. Sure, we have theories about why dogs eat grass, why tissues often seem to be a favorite item for some object guarding dogs, why dogs circle before lying down, what causes canine thunder phobia, but no one has conclusively explained why dogs engage in these behaviors. The only way we'd know for sure is to spend time being a dog. Given much of what I've seen from my dog, that probably wouldn't help either as I'm fairly certain she too doesn't know why she does some of what she does.

Robert Terson, author of *Selling Fearlessly,* notes about sales: "It won't become instinctive overnight, but given enough time and experience it'll happen. What isn't intuitive today soon will be, if you're determined enough to make it happen" (Terson, 2012).

I don't think I can sell. This is very often the initial emotion of anyone faced with selling. As noted earlier, the sales process may feel far from a natural one. Trying to motivate a total stranger to purchase your services is not an easy task. Every salesperson has struggled with this. Feeling like you can't sell isn't unusual. How you negotiate that fear is critical. The future of your business hinges on how you respond to this self-doubt and anxiety.

I can't sell. As noted earlier, this feeling is often rooted in the assumption that the ability to sell is a native skill rather than an acquired one. We can all be productive salespeople if we invest the time to learn the necessary skills. The danger in not believing this is that often it leads to a mindset of "I can't do it, so why bother trying?" Sadly, it's just not true. You *can* sell.

I don't need to sell. Many trainers rationalize away the need to sell. They often convince themselves that their website, social media, etc. will sell for them. While these are all very important components of the sales process, they're nothing more than tools. They don't replace the need for direct communication with a prospective client.

I would never sell—selling is for manipulators and exploiters. Frequently I encounter trainers who take a borderline self-righteous stance against the sales process. I have learned that typically, the more adamant someone is in their negativity about selling, the more likely that opinion is rooted in fear and self-doubt. The level to which someone resists is often in direct correlation to the level of anxiety s/he is experiencing.

When I was a kid, I had a teacher who used to say "If it's worth doing, it's worth doing really poorly while you struggle to learn how to do it well." If you want your business to thrive, and if you want to help dogs and their owners, selling is clearly worth doing. That said, learning how to sell is actually a lot easier than you might think. In all my years in sales management, I can't think of a single person of whom I would have said, "This person will never learn how to sell" because saying so would be the equivalent of saying, "This person will never survive in this world." We're all selling (persuading) all day long. It's vital to our survival. But more on that later!

Remember, you can choose not to be "that kind" of a salesperson

A few years ago I met Matt OBrien, an employee at a dog shelter. He was one of the key people who cared for the dogs in residence, including one I would eventually adopt. My dog Pepper, who lived at that shelter for almost two years, and I are eternally grateful to Matt.

Over time, I built a friendship with Matt. One day while we were chatting, I mentioned that he had the makings of a great trainer.

"I don't have the stomach to be a dog trainer" was his response.

Not understanding, I asked him to explain his comment.

It turned out that all Matt knew about training was what he had seen practiced by the facility's heavy-handed trainer. He assumed that what he had witnessed were the methods used by all trainers. He cared far too much for dogs to ever practice those techniques.

The next time I saw him, I gave Matt a few books written by leading trainers in the field of positive reinforcement training. From that point forward, we discussed training every time we saw each other. He was like a sponge, absorbing new information about a methodology he never knew existed.

Better still, he has utilized what he learned to enrich the lives of countless dogs in his care.

Please be very careful about characterizing the sales process as one only practiced by shiftless manipulators. As demonstrated with Matt OBrien's story, don't let *your* personal experience with a few con artists (*professional* salespeople are not con artists) color your view of an entire profession.

I know I've already mentioned this and you haven't read the last of it because I can't make this point strongly enough, *the goal of a professional salesperson is to help others*, not take advantage of them. Just because some people do try to exploit customers, just as some trainers are abusive to dogs, doesn't mean you need to act in the same manner.

In *Selling Fearlessly*, Robert Terson notes "There are 'salespeople' who are but a step above the con artist. They're not there to serve people; they're there to milk them. They're not there to provide value, the hallmark of the professional salesperson. Their chutzpah, silver tongues, and power of persuasion churn out positive results—for themselves only; for a while anyway. These 'salespeople' give the selling profession a bad name. It doesn't have to be this way, and you don't have to be exploitive to be successful. You'll make more money and be a lot happier with

ook into Petsmart facebook
oblem

- Grooming Tools with a retail of $10 or more.
- Filters and pumps with a retail of $10 or more.
- Pet Medications / Vitamins with a retail of $10 o
- K-9 Advantix, Advantage and Frontline Flea and Tick pro

Return Policy

We will gladly accept returns on merchandise 60 days of the original purchase date. Items m re-saleable and returned in original packaging all parts included.

With a Receipt

If original purchase was made with:	Refund given as:
Cash	Cash
Charge Card	Credit to Card
Check, within 10 days	Merchandise Return C
Check, after 10 days	Cash
Debit Card	Cash
PetSmart Gift Card	Merchandise Return C
All other gift cards	Cash
Merchandise Credit	Merchandise Return C
Traveler's Cheque	Cash
Gift Receipt	Merchandise Return C
Petsmart.com	Original Card or Merchandise Return C
Other Retailers	Merchandise Return C

Without a Receipt / Receipt Older than 60 Da

- Valid ID required

yourself if you put the customer's needs and welfare above your own" (Terson, 2012).

When I lecture, I always ask my audience: "How many of you have a positive association with the word 'selling'?" My hunch is that I'd get the same response if I asked: "How many of you have a positive association with the word 'taxes'?" Then I ask, "How many of you have a positive association with the words 'dog training'?" A sea of hands rise.

My next questions are, "Isn't there just as high a percentage of incompetent, unethical individuals in each field? Why have you made a distinction between the two professions?" I find it even more puzzling that many dog trainers, people who make their living motivating and persuading dogs *and* humans, have a strong negative association to the sales process. What is selling, if not motivating and persuading?

Perhaps the root for the –CER toward the sales process can be found in how the average person defines a salesperson. Too many think salespeople make their living by misleading, playing shell games, and engaging in various appalling acts of trickery in order to scam people to part with their hard-earned money for something that they never wanted to begin with. If only Arthur Miller had written "Death of a Podiatrist."

Just as we might instruct a dog owner to change a cue word once it has been poisoned, we should change the "salesperson" label to "compliance specialist" or "persuasion engineer" or better still, "helper"—call it what you may, it's the same process.

I recently heard a radio commercial for a jewelry store that stated, "…and don't worry about a salesperson trying to sell you something you don't want. That won't happen in our store." The commercial identifies salespeople by the lowest common denominator. It's no different than Breed Specific Legislation in which the dog, rather than the owner, is labeled as the problem. *Selling* isn't the problem, the perpetrator of the methods *used to con rather than help* is the problem.

We're all aware of dog trainers who are incompetent, unprofessional, uninformed and, in some cases, lacking in ethics. However, we don't broadly brush the entire profession negatively because of them. Instead, our association with the words "dog training" remains positive. We continue to train and see what we do, justifiably, as being of great value.

In fact, because we're proud of our profession and want to show dog owners just how wonderful training can be, those "bad" trainers often inspire us to be even better trainers than we already are.

Similarly, I invite you to be motivated as a professional salesperson in part *because* of those who are utilizing less than ethical sales methods. You can choose to be whatever type of salesperson you desire to be. I did and I wouldn't change one minute of my 23 years in sales—it has been a most gratifying journey and along the way I have built some cherished relationships.

You might have had some unpleasant experiences with "salespeople," but this doesn't mean that anyone who engages in selling is unscrupulous and that if you engage in the sales process, you are as well. As noted by Maya Angelou, "You may not control all the events that happen to you, but you can decide not to be reduced by them."

You can be a salesperson and still be a caring, decent, honest and respected human being. I invite you join the ranks of professional salespeople who understand their job is to *help* people. Once you toss aside some preconceived notions about selling (as Matt OBrien did with his feelings about dog trainers) you too will be able to enrich the lives of countless dogs and their owners.

If you help, all good things will follow—and clients will find you

Continuing with the concept of the salesperson as helper, if you help, good things happen.

Former Dallas Cowboy star Thomas Hollywood Henderson tells this story when presenting inspirational lectures to recovering drug addicts. He calls it "Who will find you?" The story can be applied to any walk of life. When you help people, they'll come back to help you.

> *Two men were enjoying a relaxing day while fishing off their sailboat when, within the blink of an eye, a huge storm rolled in and knocked them some 1,200 miles off course to a deserted island.*
>
> *In the hopes of being rescued, upon crawling out of the boat, one of the men immediately began to build a fire and write "HELP" in the sand.*
>
> *The other man calmly watched while sitting under the shade of a tree.*

> *Noticing this, his friend ran over and exclaimed, "Why are you just sitting there, aren't you going to help me!? We'll die here if no one finds us!"*

> *Calmly, his friend waved his hand and responded, "For the past ten years, I have made $1 million a year and each one of those years I donated $50,000 to my pastor's church."*
>
> *"What on earth has that got to do with this!?" replied his increasingly agitated friend.*
>
> *"Well" his buddy said as he calmly stretched and leaned his back to the tree, "my pastor is going to find me."*

You are in the *helping* business. A maxim of the great sales consultant and motivational speaker Zig Ziglar was: "You can get all you want in life if you'll help enough other people get what they want." That is, if you simply choose to help others, without ulterior motives, good things will come in return (Ziglar, 2007).

The next time training prospects ring your phone, or send you email inquiries, forget about selling to those dog owners and remember, there's a reason they contacted you—they need your help. Help and good things will follow. Help as much as you can. Help without the expectation of receiving something in return and you'll be amazed at how often you *will* receive something in return.

4

The Key Components of Successful Selling

The first step toward effective selling is to define your product or, more accurately stated, to know what your client is purchasing. Here are the key components of product knowledge and how to get that product in the hands of as many people as possible:

1. What's your line?
2. Creating value by selling benefits.
3. Pricing your services.
4. You are your client's first purchase.
5. Differentiating your services.
6. Turning your clients into salespeople for you.

Let's examine each in detail.

1. What's your line?

What's My Line was a TV game show that ran in the United States from 1950 to 1967. The game challenged celebrity panelists to determine the occupation of contestants by asking a series questions within a time limit.

For the purposes of this book, this show's contestant is a fellow named Christopher Columbus. If you guessed that his expert occupation was explorer, you were incorrect. As an explorer, Columbus missed his target by 12,000 miles. He substantially underestimated the size of the earth and substantially overestimated the size of Asia.

That said, Columbus, the salesperson, was par excellence. For seven years he hawked his idea—a shorter trip to the spice-rich East Indies—to the leaders of Portugal, England, Venice, Genoa, and Spain. And for seven years, he was rejected, until mounting competition in the European spice market and the need for a shorter, less expensive route to the East Indies, led to Spain's acceptance of his plan.

Before he could make his journey, just as every good salesperson does, Christopher Columbus convinced his investors he could solve their needs. His real job title was, "Salesperson, solving problems through exploration."

What's *your* line? If you see your title as "dog trainer," I think, similar to Columbus, you're heading in the wrong direction. Instead, I'd suggest that you see yourself as "salesperson, selling dog training expertise in order to solve or prevent a problem."

The difference between the two is critical. One title—"dog trainer"—immediately places you in a reactive mode, waiting for the business to come to you. The other title clearly suggests that you need to be proactive in acquiring sales. Additionally, the second title also makes it clear that you're not selling *sit, down, stay*, and other obedience cues. Rather, you're solving a problem. You're selling a better quality of life for the owner and the dog. If you see your product in this light, you'll more easily and effectively be able to communicate what your business provides. Your business doesn't sell obedience cues, it sells an improved quality of life. That's pretty darn impressive.

Ilya Pozin in his article "*9 Biggest Mistakes Entrepreneurs Make,*" notes astutely that "Far too many entrepreneurs think their outstanding idea will sell itself—and they couldn't be further from the truth." Pozin's point is clear; selling is a proactive, not passive, activity. You might possess excellent dog training skills, but they won't "self-sell" (Pozin, 2013).

The first step toward helping a client purchase your skills is the recognition that you're a *salesperson*. If that feels a bit out of reach, keep in mind that we can always change our perceptions. When we change our self-concept, our subconscious minds change accordingly in order to fulfill that vision. In a sense, we are what we think and our behavior follows our perceptions. Dog training is the tool you use to deliver the product your client wishes to purchase. Your primary job is selling that tool.

Let's say if someone at a social function solicited your advice regarding an issue she was having with her dog, you'd likely be comfortable with the content of the ensuing discussion. The conversation would probably be stress free, and your comfort level, in terms of your ability to provide useful information, would be high. And yet, when that same conversation occurs with a prospective client during a sales call, your state of mind and emotions are often different. The only difference is your perspective:

> *I was scared to death of the sales aspect of my business. I knew I wanted to train dogs, but I also knew I had to sell and prove my value before I could get into the home to train! I would always feel like a used car salesman trying to make a deal, but I learned that my job is to help owners solve their problems. As soon as I took the money out of the equation and focused on simply helping, the sales part became so much easier. Now, I am able to 'sell' my services without the guilt and uncomfortable nature of money. I now know their money will bring positive changes in their lives and their dog's life for years to come.*
> Mary Jean Alsina, owner of The Canine Cure, LLC.

The sales process is simply one person collecting information and then providing a product or service to help solve another person's problem. When you are hyper focused on the fact that you are *selling*, the pressure that accompanies this fixation is often the very thing assuring that you won't make the sale. Minimize pressure by reminding yourself that you are *helping* people to solve problems.

2. Creating value by selling benefits

"Che diavolo!" (Loosely translated as What the Hell!) exclaimed the barber noticing a storefront window sign that proclaimed, in large black letters: "HAIRCUTS—ONE DOLLAR."

In the 1920s, my grandfather owned a small barber shop in Brooklyn located one block down from the storefront displaying the one dollar haircut sign. It turned out that one of my grandfather's competitors had sold his business to a new (and much younger) barber. The problem was my grandfather had always charged $1.25 for haircuts, and back then 25 cents was no laughing matter. Turning on his heels and walking briskly back to his own shop, he began to consider his options—lowering his price was clearly not one of them.

So, one sunny October morning, my grandfather decided to welcome the enterprising young man to the neighborhood with a sign of his own. With a mischievous grin adorning his face, my grandfather arrived at his shop earlier than usual. Humming one of his favorite Puccini arias, he busied himself decorating his storefront window.

When the job was complete, he dashed outside to inspect his handiwork. There, in all its glory, smack dab in the middle of the window was a multicolored sign announcing:

"WE FIX DOLLAR HAIRCUTS"

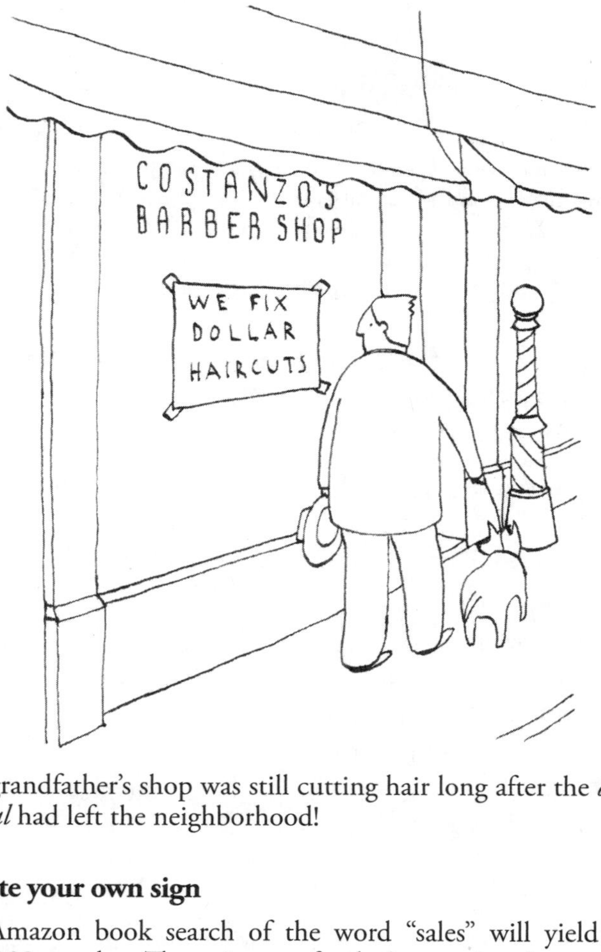

My grandfather's shop was still cutting hair long after the *dollar special* had left the neighborhood!

Create your own sign

An Amazon book search of the word "sales" will yield over 300,000 results. The science of sales/persuasion is a widely researched and extensively covered topic.

Yet, in just four words, my grandfather captured much of what these books teach and what we'll cover in the upcoming pages:

- Sell value added benefits, not features.

- Differentiate your product.
- Put your competition on the defensive.
- Emotionally engage your prospect.
- Paint a visual.
- Make all of the above memorable.

You can create a concise, memorable, inspiring sales presentation for your dog training business just as my grandfather did for his business. With a little imagination and some focused crafting of your message, you can fashion the equivalent of a "We fix dollar trainers" benefits statement for your business.

Features versus benefits—don't be a teller, be a seller.

I would like to sell you my new invention. It's called a smart phone. Following are the selling points:

- Display: Super AMOLED HD Display, 720p (720 x 1280)
- Stereo Bluetooth Class 1, Version 4.0 LE + EDR
- 4G Mobile Memory 12
- 1GB RAM x 16 GB ROM, 12 GB user available memory expandable with microSD card
- Materials and finish: Scratch-resistant display with splash guard protection

The problem with these selling points is that they're nothing more than a listing of *features*. Features don't engage the potential buyer's emotions. Features don't paint a visual. Features don't answer the customer's question, "What's in it for me?"

On the other hand, would you feel more motivated to purchase my invention if I presented these selling points?

- Freedom to leave your home or office and still be able to stay in contact (via voice conversation or emails) with family, friends, and customers.

- Communicate with anyone from anywhere at any time via text messages, emails, social media, and voice.
- Stay in touch during family or work emergencies.
- Utilize your time more effectively.
- Feel peace of mind, safety, and security knowing your phone's GPS system will prevent you from getting lost.

A feature is a description of what your product or service does for the buyer. It is a characteristic that is objective, quantifiable, and irrefutable. While features are accurate facts, they don't communicate how they will help the potential buyer.

With that said, features are important. It's helpful if your customer knows the basic facts about what you're offering (especially how you'll be motivating her dog through positive reinforcement). But features typically don't make or break a sale. When selling to a potential client, it's the *benefits* of those features that will ultimately persuade the client. And presenting them in the right light can mean the difference between gaining and losing a customer.

Unlike features, a benefit is a statement about value or usefulness. If we see the feature as a tool, the benefit is what can be achieved with that tool. Customers are looking for solutions, and a benefit shows the customer how your features will solve their problems or ease their pain.

Benefits typically:

- Save money
- Save time
- Reduce stress
- Reduce effort
- Eliminate fear
- Increase confidence
- Increase satisfaction/happiness
- Provide freedom

- Eliminate frustration
- Provide peace of mind
- Make clients feel more in control

As has been often stated: "Features tell, benefits sell."

Customers don't always know what they want

The saying, "The customer is always right," was coined in 1909 by Harry Gordon Selfridge, the founder of Selfridge's department store in London. While the accuracy of this statement can be debated (I personally think the burger had fallen off Mr. Selfridge's bun), if we accept it at face value, it presumes that customers always know what they're looking to purchase. That is often not the case unless the benefits of that product are spelled out for them. We frequently need to define our product in clear, benefit-driven terms as recounted to me in this example when I was a novice salesperson:

A person goes into a tire shop to purchase two tires. He recounts a story about how two tires were stolen from his car and how upset he is about how easily it happened. The salesperson commiserates, sells him two new tires and then inquires, "Is there anything else I can help you with?" The customer responds that he has purchased what he needs, thanks him, and heads for the door. As he is leaving, the store manager asks him if he was satisfied with his shopping experience. The customer responds that indeed, he was and then proceeds to tell the manager about the tires that were stolen from his car. The manager responds, "Did you know you can purchase wheel locks for those tires?" Fifteen minutes later, knowing that he'd never again have to worry about tires being stolen from his vehicle, a very happy customer leaves the store. As he drives away, the manager approaches the salesperson and asks, "Why didn't you sell him the wheel locks?" "He didn't ask for them" replied the salesperson.

This salesperson didn't understand that the benefit the customer was looking to purchase was peace of mind. It took the store manager's questions to bring the salesperson and the customer to this realization. More often than not, there is an emotional component driving a customer's purchase decision. Studies performed utilizing functional magnetic resonance imaging machines, which measure brain activity by detecting associated changes in blood flow to activated areas of the brain, have shown conclusively that often buyers are initially driven by emotion and then utilize logic to justify his or her purchase decisions. In many cases, the client isn't aware of the underlying emotions driving their decision.

As Henry Ford famously said of his customers: "If I had asked people what they wanted, they would have said faster horses!"

Help your prospective clients by clearly spelling out the benefits that can be gained through your training services. Think the way your clients think. Walk in their shoes and add value to your transactions by proactively addressing needs they might not even be aware of. Your chances for success will increase if you think like a salesperson. Your chances for success will increase *dramatically* if you think like a client.

How your business can benefit from benefits

What if you used the same approach when selling your services? For example, instead of just saying that you'll be teaching a "drop" cue so that the dog will drop an item when cued to do so, you note the benefits of the cue in this manner:

- Not chasing after your dog when he takes an item reduces the chances of your dog stealing (and possibly destroying) items in order to get your attention.
- Reduce the risk of object guarding aggression by teaching your dog that dropping an item is in his best interest.
- Reduce the chances of your dog ingesting an item that could result in a substantial vet bill or worse.

Don't assume your prospects know what can be achieved by hiring you. Always think of ways to communicate benefits that motivate, engage emotionally, and paint a picture. Emotional engagement causes people to act—bland statements about features don't.

A potential client's ultimate purchase decision is based on self-interest: "I want this." Better still: "I need this." Or: "This is good for me." That's all about emotions and nothing touches a client's emotions more effectively than well-crafted benefit statements.

Elevator down—how to identify benefits

That "B" that you see on the elevator control panel doesn't stand for "basement," it stands for "benefits."

There's a little exercise I perform when converting feature statements into benefits. I picture myself getting onto a "benefits" elevator. In front of me is the elevator control panel. I make a statement about my services and then I add this question, "Which means?" After each new statement, I see the elevator panel light up at the next level down and then, I repeat the process. When I am sure the elevator is at the basement level, I know I have identified a benefit.

Example: Let's say you're interested in purchasing a car, and I'm your salesperson. I might inform you, "This vehicle is powered by a four-wheel drive system." That's a feature statement that needs to be converted to a benefit statement. So I ask myself:

Which means? "The transmission provides power directly to all four wheels of the vehicle."

Which means? "All the wheels are powered, providing more stability and power."

Which means? "You'll have more control while driving in bad weather."

Which means? "You're less likely to have an accident while driving in bad weather."

Which means? "You and other family members will have peace of mind knowing you're all safe while driving in bad weather."

Take a look at where we started, "This vehicle is powered by a four-wheel drive system." and where we ended, "You and other family members will have peace of mind knowing you're all safe while driving in bad weather." Which statement is more compelling? Which statement is more likely to motivate the potential buyer to act? Remember, features tell, but benefits sell.

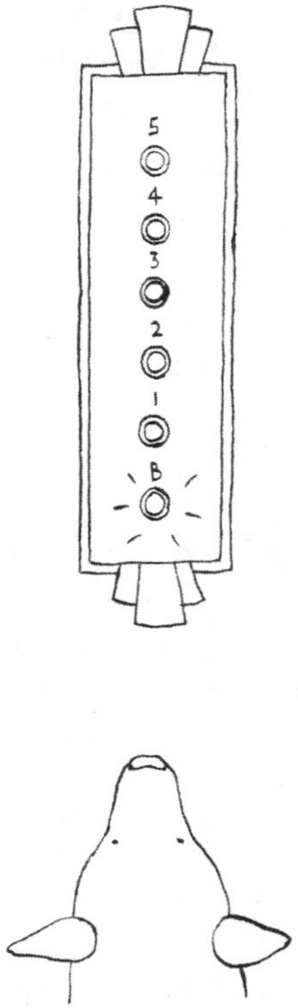

Now let's do the same exercise with your product. For this example, I'll use a solid recall behavior as the product.

"We will teach your dog a recall cue."

Which means? "Your dog will learn to come when called."

Which means? "Your dog will respond when off leash."

Which means? "Your dog will respond at a distance."

Which means? "Your dog will be under control, even at a distance."

Which means? "You will be able to keep your dog out of harm's way, even at a distance."

Which means? "You'll have peace of mind knowing that if your dog is about to get into trouble while at a distance, you'll be able to keep her/him from harm."

We have just reached the "B" level on the control panel.

When you talk with the prospect, paint the picture, "If your dog happens to bolt out the front door toward the street, you'll have peace of mind knowing that by using your recall cue, you'll be able to keep your dog from harm." That's a lot more compelling than, "We'll teach your dog a recall cue." Visuals that express benefits engage a person's emotions and motivate them to act.

Steve Jobs knew the value of communicating product benefits that painted a picture and engaged the potential customer emotionally. While all other manufactures of MP3 players were stating "1GB storage on your MP3 player," Apple's ads showed a picture of their product with a simple statement next to it, "1,000 songs in your pocket." Apple's competitor's products were essentially the same—the presentation completely different. And we all know who won that competition.

Benefit statements motivate buyers.

Put your business on "auto-sell" by selling experiences

From his window seat in a diner, my Uncle Bob admired the new sports car. He pictured himself driving along with the top down, waving to friends and neighbors. He had already measured the trunk to make sure it was big enough to store his guitar and ampli-

fier and could only imagine how cool he would look pulling up to his gigs in this sporty red beauty.

Years ago, my uncle was shopping for a new car. While at a dealership, he found himself extremely attracted to a red convertible in the showroom. Casually walking over, so as not to alert the salesman (yes, believe it or not, I have a sales aversive uncle), he checked out the pricing on the car's window sticker. In spite of the fact that he knew his bank account would strenuously object, he ran through some calculations in his mind. By then, the salesman had approached.

"Beautiful car, isn't it?" he said, pointing out the obvious. Oh, how Uncle Bob envisioned the dozens of times he'd hear that very same comment if he owned this crimson baby.

"Yeah, it's a beauty alright, but so is the price tag," responded my smitten uncle.

After chatting with the salesperson for a few minutes, with his better judgment assuming control, he commented, "Thanks. I'll think about it. Is there a good local place for lunch?"

"Sure. There's a great diner just down the road. Tell you what, take the car so that you can think about it without the pressure of me standing next to you." Without waiting for a response from my uncle, the salesman handed him the keys.

My uncle drove off the lot, arrived at the diner, parked that red beauty right out front and gazed at it for an hour while eating lunch. A brand new red sports car was sold that day without the salesman even being present. From his diner window seat, my uncle *sold himself* the car while he admired it and envisioned it parked in his driveway.

That's the power of selling an experience.

When the Connecticut School of Broadcasting sells their product, a career in the field of sports broadcasting, the experience is what they highlight. Here is sales copy from one of their ads:

> *When you work in sports broadcasting, going behind the scenes of a professional sporting event is just part of your job. Imagine the excitement of working before a camera on the sidelines of a pro football game, interviewing one of your favorite players, or hearing your voice echo through a stadium full of thousands of screaming fans! We can provide you with the hands-on training you need to make it happen.*

Notice how the ad doesn't mention a single word about compensation. Instead, they are selling the experience.

Sell the experience of living with a well trained dog

"When we're done, you and I are going to throw out that bottle of Nature's Miracle together. Won't *that* be fun?" That's the *experience* I sell when I discuss house training with a prospective customer. "Imagine living with a dog who sits, rather than barks, for attention." The idea is to put the prospect in the driver's seat as, quite literally, the car salesman accomplished with my uncle.

Help potential clients visualize the experiences they can enjoy by allowing you to help them.

A few years ago, I conducted an in-home training session for a family with a Goldendoodle puppy. As I coached the owners on a few obedience cues, their five-year-old daughter busied herself painting a picture on a canvas that was perched on an easel. Occasionally, I would invite her to help us with the puppy, which she did with delight before going back to her painting.

At the end of the session, she approached me and said, "Thank you for making our GoldenNoodle a better dog. This is for you." And she handed me the painting. I went home, framed the picture and hung it up in my office. While looking at it a few days later, I was thinking of what that little girl's experience would have been if I was a force trainer. At that moment it occurred to me that her painting could help potential clients understand what the experience of working with me would feel like. Now, when I send a follow up email after an initial chat with a prospective client, along with a list of my certifications, I attach a scan of the painting and a short description about how it was created.

As accurately noted in Steve W. Martin's book *Heavy Hitter Sales Linguistics*, "You need to package these ideas in a format that leaves an impression and creates a call to action that customers understand and that persuades them both mentally and emotionally to proceed" (Martin, 2011).

Think about how you can communicate experiences to your prospects and clients via words that create visuals. Paint a picture that appeals to the client's emotions and creates a call to action.

3. Pricing your services

Every price is too high…until the client sees the benefits and value in your services.

For which would you be willing to spend more money, a parachute or a Mercedes? If you are safely on the ground examining the price of each item, the answer is a no-brainer. But if you're about to jump out of a plane, I think you'd agree the parachute would have more value.

Customers perceive value based on their needs and how well your product solves their problems.

When selling, many dog trainers fall into the trap of being fretfully fixated on the price they charge. Often, price is a bigger problem for the trainer than it is for the prospect. True, at the inception of most sales calls, the customer's focus is on *price*. As the sales process continues, it is your goal to refocus the customer's attention on *value*.

Oscar Wilde once said, "The cynic knows the price of everything and the value of nothing." Well, maybe the cynic didn't have a good salesperson.

When you are selling your services, you need to know how well you have answered the prospective client's underlying question:

"What's in it for me?" When you answer that question, you have defined value and shifted the focus from price to value.

What is the cost/benefit ratio of hiring you? On one side of the scale, the prospect sees your price, and on the other side is the perceived value of your services. Note that I use the words "perceived value" because the value of the services you offer are not actually *in* your product, but are instead *in the mind* of the prospect. It is important to understand that often value is a need-based perception that differs from person to person. Value is not an absolute.

Your goal is to make sure the scale is weighed down on the benefit/value side. There are two ways to achieve this: lower your price or raise the value of the benefits for your prospect. As you've already learned, I am not a fan of lowering prices. You've worked hard to obtain your training skills, you're providing your customer with amazingly high value—you deserve to be well compensated.

The truth is that nobody would buy any product or service—regardless of the price—if they didn't perceive value. Value and price are two very different things. If they were the same, no one would buy a Gibson Guitar, a Lexus automobile, or a Gucci bag. The only time that a product or service absolutely needs to be cheaper than a competitor is when it is considered to be a commodity, that is, when it has no other point of differentiation other than price.

It is of critical importance that you prevent your training business from being seen as a commodity. In order to avoid this, you must create value in the minds of your prospective clients. The first step in value creation is to understand what it is your client is looking to purchase and then spell out the benefits of your services with regard to their desires.

Don't underestimate the value you provide

Noted sales guru Zig Ziglar used to ask a series of questions as a way of showing his audience the value of the product they were selling. I present them here tailored specifically to dog trainers:

> *Do you still have every dollar you've earned through dog training?* I didn't think so. In fact, I'd be willing to bet a shiny nickel that in several cases, you had already spent some portion (or all) of your fees prior to arriving at the training appointment.
>
> *Do your clients still benefit today from the training services you provided last year, two years ago, even ten years ago?* You bet they do.
>
> *Who made the better deal, you or your client?* Your clients are still benefiting today from services you provided years ago. In fact, they can transfer those benefits to every dog they'll own for the rest of their lives. Your product comes with a wide range of uses and no expiration date. Sounds like you're selling a darn good product!

Don't underestimate the value of your product. When we don't embrace the value and benefits of our services, we often feel discomfort in asking for appropriate compensation and so we price our services too low. If you spread the cost of your services over the lifetime of your client's dog, the investment is literally pennies per day. More importantly, if cost is measured by the daily negative consequences caused by a poorly trained dog, the cost of *not* training substantially outweighs your price *for* training. And as noted above, you're selling an enriched quality of life—what could be more valuable than that?

Clients are paying for your knowledge, not your time. Take a moment to consider all the time you've invested learning your trade and the financial investments you've made along the way. Realistically, you're more financially limited by what your market might bear than you are by your value. Be proud of what you provide to dog owners, and don't undervalue yourself.

Not sure what to charge? It's like pricing fish in a barrel

When my grandfather was a kid, he worked in a fish market at the South Street Seaport in New York City. One day the owner of the store wheeled out two barrels from a storage room. He positioned both barrels near the checkout counter. With a wave of his hand, he summoned my grandfather. Pointing to a large wooden crate across the store he instructed, "I want you to take that delivery of fish and count out an even amount to place in each barrel. Then, by one barrel place a sign, 'Fish: 19 cents per pound' and by the other barrel, a sign that says 'Fish: 24 cents per pound.'"

At the turn of the 20th century, kids didn't question authority, but my grandfather couldn't resist. "But the fish are the same for each barrel," he noted sheepishly. "One barrel is for people who want better fish," grumbled the store owner as he walked away.

At the conclusion of each business day, the cantankerous store owner instructed my grandfather to count the number of fish left in each barrel. If there were fewer fish in the 24 cent barrel, my grandfather was instructed to raise the price by one cent for that barrel. The fish were again evenly distributed in each barrel and offered for sale.

This process was repeated each day until the less expensive barrel outsold the more expensive barrel. When that occurred, the pricing for the more expensive barrel was brought back to the prior day's price.

In his own very unscientific manner, the store owner was executing a pricing philosophy with which I concur—if you're not receiving objections based on price, you're not charging enough.

Too high or too low—how do you know?

Determining pricing, while important, isn't as complex as some people make it out to be. If you are often receiving price objections, it is vitally important that you *first* review your sales presentation to ensure that you are presenting enough value for your prospective clients. Remember, until you create value, price is what customers will be focused on.

If you're presentation is outstanding, and you are still receiving rejections based on price, then it's possible you've exceeded the price ceiling for your services. If you are not receiving objections/rejections due to your pricing, chances are you're not charging enough.

Yes, I know it feels like this should be a much more complex matter. It isn't.

4. *You* are your client's first purchase

My close friend Bill is an art teacher. For the past 30 years, at the start of each school year, he has used the same introduction with his students. Bill understands that *teaching is selling*. In order to persuade his students to follow his coaching, he must first win them over. On that first day, most children would much prefer to see a young female teacher walk into their classroom than

Bill who is a tall, dark-haired, mustachioed, deep-voiced man. With an awareness of how children might be intimidated by his appearance, his first question of these 10-year-old children is, "So, how many of you got married over the summer?"

Lots of giggles ensue, and a few mischievous souls raise their hands, to which Bill responds, "First marriage?"

Now that he has warmed them up a bit, he mentions their first lesson topic will be about color and he makes sure the next question he asks can't be answered incorrectly: "What's your favorite color?"

Bill is a smart fellow. He understands the value of selling *himself* first and then creating a positive initial experience by asking a question that can't possibly have an incorrect answer. He's also crafty enough to ask an open-ended question that can lead to discussion rather than a yes or no question.

With the initial goal of selling *himself* accomplished, the process of persuading his students is markedly easier.

In the field of car sales, when asked about the value of a trade-in vehicle, car salespeople are taught to use that vehicle for the gathering of information. They're not looking *at* the car, they're looking *inside* the car. Is there a car seat inside? A case for a musical instrument? Fishing pole? Golf balls? A book?

Any information that can provide an insight into the preferences of the prospect allows the salesperson to connect personally. People prefer to say "yes" to people they like, and there's no one we like more than someone who is similar to us.

From Steve W. Martin's *Heavy Hitter Sales Linguistics*: "The sales call involves the process of building a relationship by turning a stranger into a friend and a skeptic into a believer. The first step in the process is to establish mutual trust in which both parties are assured of the competence of each other. Finally, developing rapport by connecting with the customer is your top priority in every conversation with the customer. The sale won't happen without rapport" (Martin, 2011).

Once a rapport and comfort level has been established, it makes the sales process infinitely easier. Try not to lose sight of the fact that just as Bill's young students see him as an authority figure, your prospect sees you as an authority and will often feel some level of discomfort during the early moments of your initial conversation. Additionally, dog owners very frequently see their dog's behavior as a self-reflection. When they feel overwhelmed with the daunting task of training their dog, the very act of calling you might be accompanied by a sense of failure.

It's time to lighten the load by helping them to develop a sense of comfort with you. As early as possible, I make it a point to ask, "What's your dog's name?" and "Why did you choose that name?" Just like Bill's "What's your favorite color?" question, it's an inquiry that can't be answered incorrectly and it helps the caller to connect with me on a person-to-person level, rather than as teacher and student. And the ensuing discussion is always fun.

I have a page on my website, "Pepper, my rescue dog." The page is there because quite frankly, I'm madly in love with my dog. I didn't create it as a sales tool. Yet, it's amazing how many prospective customers read the story about her life (it's the most popular page on my site) and talk to me about it during our initial conversation. When they do, we've connected as dog owners rather than an authority figure and student.

When I am speaking with owners who are experiencing garden variety training issues, I immediately level the playing field by making them feel at ease: "So nice to know that I'm not the only one who's had that experience. My dog used to do the same thing." And then I tell them a quick story to illustrate that I can relate. By doing so, I have provided a sense of comfort because I have informed them that not only can I understand their issue, but I have worked through the same issue(s) with my dog. I'm "fortunate" because Pepper had just about every behavioral issue known to mankind so I have a quick and easy reference at my disposal. If I didn't, I'd simply cite my work with another dog as an example. The goal is to set the prospective client at ease and to a degree, normalize (yes other dogs jump on guests, counter surf, bark, etc.) the behaviors they are looking to modify.

Obviously, if the owner has called about a dog who has bitten, or shown aggression, this is not the time for being lighthearted. But with that said, I often mention that Pepper bit me twice within the first week after I rescued her from two years of shelter life. The dog owner in me wants to let the caller know that I truly understand how upsetting the experience can be.

In all cases, try to make sure you first connect as a dog owner, not a dog trainer. Make an effort to communicate your appreciation for their problem with real-life examples that truly illustrate an understanding of their struggles. The more someone can identify with you, the more likely their barriers will come down, the more they'll see you as similar to them, the more they'll like you, the more their trust will build and the more they'll likely they'll give you the opportunity to help them by hiring you. In her book *Whoever Tells the Best Story Wins*, Annette Simmons refers to this as an "I know what you're thinking" story (Simmons, 2007).

When prospects connect with you, it's much more difficult for them to reject your proposal, because to do so would mean to reject *you* as well. When you "attach" yourself to your proposal, your chances for success are much greater. So, trust yourself and be comfortable to be yourself. Oscar Wilde once said, "Be yourself, everyone else is already taken." You're the perfect you. It's better to be a top notch you than an imitation of someone else.

And above all, during that initial conversation, be sure to ask questions and listen as if their problem is yours—after all, you want it to be.

5. Don't compete. Differentiate.

During the 1980s, the late-night television airwaves were awash with infomercials featuring products developed by a man who was known for his catch phrase, "But wait, there's more!"

Hair in a Can, the Chop-O-Matic, the Pocket Fisherman, and the Smokeless Ashtray were just a few items offered by his more than $50 million company, Ronco. In 1995, he was the subject of a book entitled *The Salesman of the Century*, but the way I see it, entrepreneur extraordinaire Ron Popeil was the *differentiator* of the century.

Product differentiation is a concept initially proposed by Edward Chamberlin in his 1933 book, *Theory of Monopolistic Competition*. Differentiation strives to place the product in a more attractive light by showcasing its unique qualities and benefits. When successful, differentiation generates an advantage for the seller as consumers view the product as unique or superior.

I doubt a person could create a greater array of unique products than those developed by Popeil. One could say his merchandise sold itself.

The health of your business is greatly dependent upon not allowing your services to be seen as exactly the same as those offered by your competitors. When this happens, your product becomes a *commodity*, a product that is the same, regardless of who is providing it. When this occurs, the only point of differentiation is the price. Price alone is not a productive way to differentiate your business. By being clear on what makes you unique, different, or better than your competitors, you avoid being seen as a commodity. This is your unique selling proposition. If you don't have one, it's time to create one.

> *I used to think that selling dog training was all I needed. Well, so did the other 20,000 dog trainers in my area. I learned that showing clients how I stand out and what I can bring to the table that is unique to me is what I needed to focus on. Showing the client why they should choose me as their trainer and conveying what I can do differently than every other trainer out there is what makes sales.*
> Mary Jean Alsina, CPDT-KA

Be creative. Research your competition in order to identify ways to be unique. The more your product stands out, the less active selling you'll need to do. You'll stand out in the mind of your prospects, and you'll be able to charge more (yes, you deserve it) if your product doesn't look "generic."

If you can't identify any points of differentiation, create some. A great starting point is *you*. There is only one you. Carve out a niche and become the most dominant player serving that client need. A great bonus to this approach is you can often raise your prices when you specialize in this manner.

How do you find a niche? Conduct an in-depth analysis of all your competitors by answering these questions:

- What do I do that they don't do?

- What do they do that I don't do?
- What do I do better than them?
- What is different about my credentials and experience?
- If I could have my clients say one positive thing about my business, what would that be?

After completing this, take a look at the results and you'll see a pattern. The key element is that your analysis needs to be in-depth.

I recently provided sales consulting for a trainer who felt that her business was pretty much the same as her competition. In fact, it wasn't. What we found after analyzing the competition in her area was that they all scheduled their package appointments at the same time every week. If you purchased a four-session package from these trainers, you were scheduled on the same weekday at the same time for four consecutive weeks.

This trainer began advertising scheduling flexibility as one of her points of differentiation. If you purchased a package of sessions, unless it was your stated preference, the session times were not slotted in advance because, as she put it, "Life happens, and sometimes even owners with the best of intentions can't get their homework done prior to the next session. Yes, it's easier for me to slot everyone into rigid schedules but it's not easier for them." By highlighting this one point of differentiation, she experienced dramatic results.

Remember, you're not selling dog training. To paraphrase Zig Ziglar, dog training is what you do—the client purchases what you can do *for them*. One of the things you can do for them is make life less stressful and training more convenient.

There's also a wealth of information about what differentiates your business from others residing within your customer base. Survey your clients after they complete your training package. Just the fact that you are asking them to complete a performance survey will differentiate you from your competition, as the vast majority don't do this.

Ask some open-ended questions, like:

- "What about your experience was different than your expectations?"
- "Based on your experience with my business, would you be willing to recommend me to other dog owners? Why?"
- "In one sentence, please describe your experience with my company."
- "How has your relationship with your dog changed after working with me?"

You'll get a considerable amount of very useful information by asking questions like these. In fact, your clients will write your benefits statements and points of differentiation *for you.*

Note: When conducting a survey, please print the survey and mail it the analog way, through the post office, along with a self-addressed stamped envelope. And while you're at it, attach a Post-it note thanking your client for completing the survey. Studies have been conducted showing that something as simple as attaching at sticky note to a survey form will as much as double the response rate.

The same thing could be said for anything you mail to clients that requires action, including your initial proposal when they engage your services. Of course, it is important to email a proposal so that it gets there quickly, but print it out and mail it as well, with a sticky note attached expressing your gratitude. By doing so, you'll be differentiating yourself from the vast majority of trainers who don't do this. Remember, in this digital age, few people add a personal touch to their communications like hand written notes. When you do, you'll stand out from the crowd that is vying for the same business.

6. Hire your clients as salespeople

In many ways your client's decision to purchase your services is only part of the sales process. As Harvey McKay, award winning author and business consultant says, "The sale begins when the customer says yes." In order to keep your clients motivated and to also have them sing your praises to other dog owners, you'll want to make a habit of pointing out the value and benefits of the your services. I like to think of each one of my clients as potential salespeople for my training business. Every client who purchases a training package is also applying for a job as a salesperson for my training business. Referrals are the best way to gain business. No one will toot your horn louder than your satisfied customers.

Finally, remember your client's motivation isn't about "what" or "how." Many dog trainers know "what" and "how," but they'll always lose the sale to the trainer who knows "why." Once we know why a dog owner has contacted us, we are in a much better position to solve their problems, gain them as a client, keep them motivated, and earn referrals from them.

5

The Science of Human Behavior and its Relation to Successful Selling

As noted earlier, just as with dog training, the foundation for successful selling is rooted in science. Following are some key concepts that will help your build a thriving business.

1. The power of missing out on something
2. The Principle of Perceptual Contrast
3. The Principle of Social Proof
4. The Rule of Reciprocation
5. Short cuts and long results

1. The power of missing out on something

Bose, a leading-edge audio company, makes some great audio equipment. When they introduced one of their new products with an ad headline that touted its *newness*, they were shocked to see how poorly the product sold. Cleary, this was a high-end product that was better than anything else on the market. And it was loaded with *new* features.

Puzzled, the company solicited advice from Robert Cialdini, author and Regents' Professor Emeritus of Psychology and Marketing at Arizona State University, who noted that "new" often only points out the risky and unproven nature of something, frequently at a time when the buyer is craving a proven, predictable product. He also explained that a more productive strategy for persuasion is to honestly inform people what they stand to lose if they don't own your product (Cialdini, 2009).

When Bose changed its ad headline from "New" to "Hear what you've been missing," it redirected people to focus on the aversion of missing out rather than the discomfort caused by the unpredictability of a new product. The result was an immediate 45 percent increase in sales.

Whenever my car is in the repair shop and I am without it for a day, I often think about all the great stuff I'm missing out on while I'm trapped in my home. Suddenly, totally insignificant items take on maximum importance merely because I'm missing out on them while sitting in my living room. Beads of sweat form on my frowning brow as I worry that Ralph's Italian Ices might have added a 117th flavor to their menu and I'm missing out on it.

The fear of missing out on something is so powerful that there's even an accepted acronym for it, FoMO. FoMO occurs when we feel that we're missing out on something more exciting, more important, or more interesting that is happening elsewhere. Studies have shown that our regrets most often center on what we didn't do, rather than on what we did. Being aware that others are doing rewarding things that we are not is fertile ground for emotional discomfort which we all want to avoid. The overwhelming popularity of social media is in great part attributable to people often checking out what's going on within their social network, lest they miss something of importance.

Show your prospective customers what they're missing out on

For your business, focus on what the dog owner (and dog) stands to lose without benefiting from your services. Paint a wonderful picture of what life *could* be as compared to what it is.

For example, you could inform dog owners about what they'll be missing out on if they don't socialize their puppy well. Or, express how children can benefit from learning how to nurture and interact with a dog and what they're missing if they don't. Or, how much fun walks can be and what the owners are missing out on if they cease walking their dog due to poor leash walking skills.

When talking with a potential client, communicate the enriched quality of life that trainers are able to visualize that many owners can't. In other words, help them to visualize and then experience what they are missing.

And be sure to mention very satisfied customers who have benefited greatly from working with you. Doing so will likely inspire your caller to feel as if s/he doesn't want to miss out on what others are enjoying—a better life gained through working with you.

2. The Principle of Perceptual Contrast

Imagine dropping your car off for a service estimate at a repair shop. The owner calls and states, "You might need an entirely new brake assembly and armature sprocket. I think there might be a problem with the Johnson rods as well. I'll call back later when I've had a chance to take a closer look." While you await the call, you're already figuring out how different life will be when you start using mass transit because there is no way you can afford such an expensive repair. A few hours later, the phone rings and the shop's owner informs you, "Hey, good news, it's only the brake pads. The entire job will cost $220." Imagine the sense of relief you'd feel when you compare the $220 to the figure you had in your head.

When presented with two things, one after another, if the second item is fairly different from the first, we will tend to see it as more different than it actually is. This is known as the Principle of Perceptual Contrast. For example, if you pick up a light object first, then a heavy one, you will estimate that the second object is heavier than if you hadn't lifted the light one first. The same thing can be made to seem very different depending on the nature of the event that precedes it.

Baseball players engage in this principle often. A batter will swing a weighted bat prior to going up to home plate to hit. Doing so makes his normal bat *feel* lighter, which makes him *feel* as if he can swing his bat faster.

A standard lab test used to demonstrate the Principle of Perceptual Contrast is to place three buckets of water—one hot, one room temperature, and one cold—in front of a subject. After placing one hand in the hot water and the other hand in the cold water, the subject is then instructed to simultaneously place both hands in the room temp water. As expected, the hand that was in the cold water experiences the room temp water as being hotter than the hand that was in the hot water, even though the hands are in the same bucket of water.

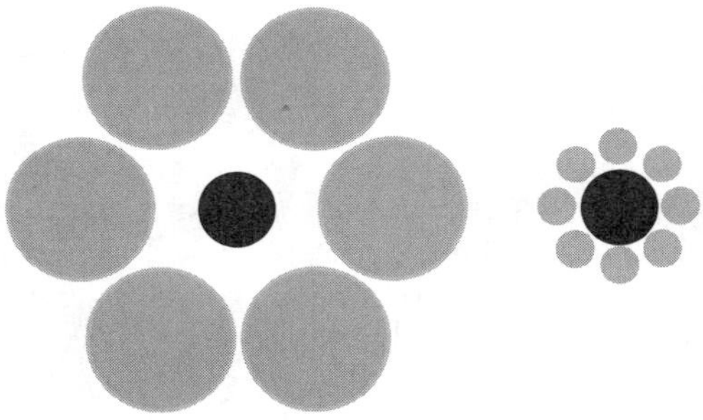

Above is an illustration of Perceptual Contrast—the center circles are actually the same size, but they don't appear to be so due to the size of the circles surrounding them.

All car dealerships rely on the Principle of Perceptual Contrast. Once the baseline price of the car has been negotiated, options are then discussed. Compared to the multi-thousand dollar price that was just negotiated for the car, the added upgrade of a GPS system...then tinted windows...then heated seats...all seem much less expensive when offered after the big ticket item, the price of the car.

We typically notice differences *between* items, not in absolute measures. The way we evaluate most things is in comparison to something else. When we say someone is funny, we usually mean that person is funnier than others. Similarly, when we make purchase decisions, we tend to do so by contrasting between items rather than against a fixed standard.

Perceptual contrast, utilized correctly, can work to your advantage.

How to utilize Perceptual Contrast effectively

Customer reliance on perceptual contrast is magnified when the aforementioned fixed standard doesn't exist, such as in the field of dog training. Consequently, since a baseline for comparison doesn't exist, clients rely more heavily on perceptual contrast to differentiate between trainers. As a salesperson, it's imperative to try to establish a fixed standard to which you will be favorably compared and to also differentiate yourself from other trainers. You can establish a fixed standard by mentioning that while the field of training is entirely unregulated, you have set a standard *for your business* that demands education, certifications, and experience. When you set this baseline successfully in the mind of your prospective client, other trainers who don't possess similar qualifications will not be seen in a favorable light.

With regard to pricing, when trainers have several packages to offer, they tend to be skittish about presenting anything but the lower priced options first. Please keep in mind while it might feel less stressful to do this, you're using the Principle of Perceptual Contrast against yourself when you do so as your higher priced options will seem even higher than they are because you've already established a lower anchor price. Because of this, not only are you less likely to sell more of your higher priced packages, you're also making the sales process more difficult for yourself.

The impact of Perceptual Contrast is one of the reasons I'm usually strongly opposed to selling consultations as a standard operating procedure. There are some instances, however, in which it does make sense. In a situation where the owner is required to make a substantial investment of time, effort, and money, or where something is unique about the context, it's advisable to provide a consultation. Separation anxiety cases are a good example. When administered correctly, the plan for behavior modification of separation anxiety entails a substantial, albeit hopefully temporary, lifestyle change for the owners. The nature of what the owner and dog are struggling with requires a longer initial discussion because gaining owner compliance can be more difficult in separation anxiety cases than with more routine training situations.

But for garden variety training requirements, such as a Lab jumping on guests, we don't need to see the dog in order to develop a training proposal. In such cases, consultations are not only unnecessary but as noted above, due to perceptual contrast, selling consultations is a counter-productive sales practice. The package you're hoping to sell costs more than the initial consultation and due to perceptual contrast, the cost will seem even greater than it actually is.

A few more words about selling consultations as a standard business procedure. A study conducted by Carnegie Mellon and Stanford Universities demonstrated conclusively that the part of our brain that responds to pain is also activated when making purchase decisions (Douley, n.d.). Buying something, regardless of how much we want the item, often causes us discomfort. When you sell a consult and then try to sell uphill for a more expensive follow-up package, not only are you going against the principle of perceptual contrast, you are activating the pain center of your prospect's brain twice—once for the initial purchase (the consult) and once for the subsequent package. Repeatedly selling single sessions is even more of an uphill struggle.

Years ago, internet service provider AOL learned how much more effective (and profitable) it was to simply charge a monthly fee rather than asking customer to pay as they surfed. When the company switched their customer payment plan, sales and profits sky rocketed.

It's also important to be mindful of the fact that your prospective client is never going to be more inspired than during that original call. You can best help by responding to that motivation by keeping the process moving steadily forward rather than breaking the momentum by selling a consultation and having to sell again (and put the dog owner through the purchase process once more) when converting to a multi-session package.

Another reason I am usually strongly opposed to selling consultations is that often, out of fear that the client might attempt a "do it yourself" solution, trainers withhold information that would help the client achieve their goals. Essentially, by withholding information, the trainer is not putting a best foot forward. Providing information, and then explaining why the client shouldn't attempt to put that information into practice without the trainer's help, is very different than purposely withholding information which, to me, feels like dishonesty by omission.

Part of my standard sales presentation includes a proactive approach to selling against any trainer who sells consults. I simply explain that my questionnaire/intake form allows me to learn about the dog, the owner's goals, and the home environment *on my own time, prior to the appointment.* I clearly and effectively make this point during the initial phone inquiry:

> *It seems to me that when a trainer charges you for a consultation, it's the same as a carpenter charging you to provide an estimate for work you want done. That doesn't seem fair to me. I don't mind investing my own time prior to our first appointment. You are a very worthwhile investment of my time. After all, without clients, I'd be out of business. I prefer to gather information through my intake form so that I don't take up your time during our first session, asking questions I could have had answered in advance while the clock is running and you're paying. And because I have reviewed your information prior to our appointment, we can hit the ground running during our first session.*

By doing this, not only have I differentiated myself from other trainers and added value to my product, I have also turned the intake form into a benefit for the client rather than a burden.

Matt Tuzzo, CTC, CPDT-KA and owner of Jersey Shore Dogs, LLC clearly expresses the downsides to selling consultations:

> *During the first one and a half years of my company's existence, I sold consultations rather than multi-session training packages. I was experiencing a fairly high level of sales call anxiety, and selling consultations felt like a more manageable middle ground. But in reality, doing so was nothing more than an avoidance behavior—one that didn't help my clients and actually made the sales process more difficult for me.*
>
> *After speaking with John, I began to only sell multi session packages and my business immediately tripled in sales when I made the switch.*
>
> *My initial phone discussion, which runs approximately 20 minutes, is easily enough time for me to sell my services. I don't need a consultation to do so. Between that call and my intake form, which clients complete prior to the first appointment, I have all the information I need about the client's needs and the dog's behavior. I don't need to see the dog in order to understand the behavioral issues and to develop a training plan.*
>
> *In the end, it's a win/win situation because I'm able to sell the entire package during one phone conversation and I'm not spending the client's money during a consultation, which in many ways is nothing more than a paid sales call, and is not a productive use of the client's money or time.*

Remember, your goal is to help the dog owner hire a trainer—you. This is most easily and effectively accomplished by selling your dog training package, once, during the initial call.

3. The Principle of Social Proof

When in unfamiliar situations and contexts, following the behaviors of others tends to limit our chances for making mistakes. We are inclined to see our behavioral choices as safe if they are similar to the behavior of those around us. This is known as the Principle of Social Proof.

"When in Rome, do as the Romans do" is more than just a saying—it's a foundational decision making tool we utilize on an almost daily basis to help us navigate through unfamiliar waters.

Social proof is a grounded, rational, adaptive behavior that is often justified by math. The more people who are doing something, the higher the probability it is the correct thing to do—or at least that it is comparatively safe. For most contexts, the Principle of Social Proof works with a high degree of reliability.

Examples of the Principle of Social Proof:

- Bartenders salt their tip jar with dollar bills in order to let patrons know that the proper tip is a paper denomination, not coins.

- Telethon hosts read the names of those who call in a pledge. The goal is to make listeners feel as if everyone is calling and that they should do likewise.
- Night club owners keep long lines at their doors even though their establishment might be empty inside. Those who pass by will think "That must be a great club, look at the line waiting to get inside."
- McDonald's displays a sign informing us of how many have been served.
- Advertisers constantly inform us about their "most talked about" or "fastest growing" products. Others are talking about the product and using it, so it must be good.

Perhaps the greatest example of social proof in practice can be found in how sales of the NordicTrac exercise equipment system increased after a simple change to their TV commercial—a change that announced to customers that they'd be inconvenienced while trying to purchase the product!

In the original commercial the announcer states, "Call now, operators are standing by." The statement draws a vision of a room full of bored order-takers staring off into space, flying paper planes, or playing hangman, while no phones are ringing.

The call to action was changed to "Call now. If operators are busy, please call again." The original visual changed from bored to busy operators, handling call after call. In fact, the company didn't even mind announcing that you might be inconvenienced because there were *that* many calls. This is a great example of social proof in action.

When people are unsure of how to act, often the deciding factor is "Others are doing it, so it must be the correct behavior. I should act accordingly."

Social proof and your training business

There are a number of ways you can utilize the Principle of Social Proof to increase your business. The key is to note examples of other dog owners who are utilizing your services and are thrilled that they have done so. Here are some examples:

- Direct your prospects to the list of testimonials on your website.
- When providing a written follow-up after a telephone sales call, do so with a few testimonials.
- Be sure to incorporate some success stories into your sales presentation. Not only will that help to paint a visual but it suggests that others are benefiting from your talents.
- Show pictures of those who have benefited from your services.
- Tell stories and present case histories of clients with whom you've had great success.
- If you've been in business for a while, mention how long your company has been around—a subtle indication of popularity.
- Cite favorable reviews provided by local newspapers/organizations.

According to a CompUSA and iPerceptions study, over 70% of Americans say they look at product reviews before making a purchase. Nearly 63% of consumers indicate they are more likely to move forward in the sales process if product ratings and reviews are available (Search Engine Journal, n.d.).

Reviews not only lend credibility to your business but they inform prospective customers that others are benefiting from your training abilities.

Be sure to incorporate Social Proof into your sales presentation: "I often work with clients who are looking to achieve the same goal as you;" "I'm more than happy to provide references;" "Just last week I worked with a dog owner who had the same issues you're looking to resolve." These are just a few examples of positive social proof statements because they communicate that others have chosen you as a trainer.

Note: When selling, be mindful of inadvertently expressing *negative* social proof in your presentation. Psychologists Noah Goldstein and Steve Martin observed the undesired effects of negative social proof with a theft prevention experiment conducted in the Arizona Petrified Forest (Goldstein, et. al., 2008). In the study, three different signs were tested, one of which included *negative* social proof: "Many past visitors have removed petrified wood from the park, destroying the natural state of the Petrified Forest." Ironically, this sign actually *increased* the likelihood that people would steal petrified wood (it tripled the amount of theft) because it was social proof that *many* past visitors had *already* stolen from the forest. Instead of discouraging people from stealing, it made them more comfortable in feeling that doing so was okay since many other people had done so. A more effective approach would have made people believe that removing petrified wood was the rarest of actions taken only by terribly uncaring individuals, of which there are fortunately few.

If during your sales presentation you state that far too many dog owners use choke collars, while your intention is good, you might be unintentionally focusing your listener on the popularity of choke collars rather than the downsides of using them and, in doing so, make it more likely that they'll hire a trainer who uses one. Just as we teach clients to reinforce desirable behaviors and ignore unwanted ones, always accentuate the positive and simply disregard the negative when looking to persuade a prospect.

4. The Rule of Reciprocation

In 1974, Dr. Phillip Kunz and his family received an above-average number of Christmas cards expressing love and affection for Phillip and his family. How wonderful it must have felt to be so loved, especially because, unlike typical holiday cards, these had been sent by total strangers. Kunz, a sociologist at Brigham

Young University, had decided to conduct an informal study to see what would happen if he sent Christmas cards to strangers. He randomly selected names, 578 in total, from listings in several local directories, and out the cards went.

Remarkably, Kunz received 117 cards in return. Several responses contained letters and handwritten notes recounting details about the sender's past year, some celebrated many years of friendship, while others wrote about their families. Only six requested additional information about the identity of the sender.

While a bit of a strange study, it nonetheless demonstrates just how powerful and influential the Rule of Reciprocation can be. Essentially, the rule states that when someone does something nice for us, we should try—in fact, we are obligated—to repay that kindness.

The Rule of Reciprocation is one of the foundational building blocks of every civilized society, and it has important adaptive significance. People can give items, services, or money knowing that they haven't diminished their resources—they are guaranteed to receive a valued item in exchange for their offering. Interestingly, sociologists have found that each and every human society, regardless of geographical location, race, or religion, follows the Rule of Reciprocity.

Each holiday season, we receive dozens of "free" pre-printed address labels (along with a donation request, of course). These labels are a wonderful example of the Rule of Reciprocation hard at work.

Robert Cialdini notes, "I can't send them back because they've got my name on them. But as soon as I've decided to keep that packet of labels, I'm in the jaws of the rule." Cialdini also notes that the "donation hit rate goes from 18 to 35 percent" when recipients receive the labels. For the cost of approximately 9 cents (the price to produce the labels), the number of people who donate almost doubles (Cialdini, 2009).

If asking clients for compensation for your services causes you discomfort, keep the Rule of Reciprocation in mind. Your clients *expect* to pay for your services. In fact, people are downright uncomfortable accepting a service without making payment in one form or another. It would be positively inconsiderate of us, really, to make clients feel uncomfortable by *not* expecting compensation for our services.

In fact, if you put on your creative thinking cap, I'm sure you can fashion a plan for giving something away to prospective clients so that the Rule of Reciprocation plays in your favor when converting prospects into customers. (Note: Do not give away your core services for free, as this only serves to devalue your product.)

Here's an interesting study conducted by Robert Cialdini:

> *A car wash ran a promotion: The customer was presented with a card which presented this offer, "Buy eight car*

washes and the next is free." Another set of customers was simultaneously offered a different promotion, "Buy ten car washes and the next is free." In this case, two car washes were already X'ed out of the tracking card. The second offer produced substantially greater results than the first. Cialdini discovered that people are inclined to complete the card more quickly and will do so with increased frequency when they feel like they have momentum toward the conclusion. People don't want to lose the advantage they started with while using the card with two Xs on it already. Additionally, with those two Xs already marked off, they have been given something for free. In this way there is a sense of reciprocity embedded within the process.

In your business, perhaps you could award a doggie toy for clients who complete four sessions, but instead of making four the qualifying number, make it six sessions, but with two already punched off the tracking card.

While the Kunz Christmas card study demonstrates the power of gifting an item, it more importantly teaches us that the anxiety associated with asking for money in exchange for training services is unnecessary. In fact, your request is as expected as a returned "good morning" when you extend a greeting to a stranger that you pass on the street.

If you don't think the Rule of Reciprocation is a strong one, consider this: For approximately 15 years, the Kunz family received Christmas cards from those strangers he contacted in 1974. Next holiday season if you'd like to receive scores of cards, just send a bunch to total strangers. Just don't try it on Phillip Kunz—he's wise to the game.

5. Shortcuts—and long results

We can apply the acronym TMI (too much information) to the amount of information that is at our disposal when we are looking to purchase a product or service. Even if we are able to conduct an extensive review of all the available data, we'd likely end up a victim of paralysis by analysis. This information glut gives rise to people relying on *shortcuts* to help them make decisions because it's simply more practical to do so. Shortcuts are what psychologists refer to as heuristics. Heuristics are simplistic rules that free us from exhausting ourselves by processing all available information. Life is too complex and complicated for people to take the time to judiciously evaluate each element of every situation prior to making a decision. Instead, we learn to take shortcuts to help us make sensible and dependable assessments and then act accordingly within those frameworks.

Robert Cialdini notes "Because of the increasing tendency for cognitive overload in our society, the prevalence of shortcut decision making is likely to increase proportionally. Although we all wish to make the most thoughtful, fully considered decision possible in any situation, the changing form and accelerating pace of modern life frequently deprive us of the proper conditions for such a careful analysis of all the relevant pros and cons. More and more, we are forced to resort to another decision-making approach—a shortcut approach" (Cialdini, 2009).

All day, every day, we make decisions. Some are as minor as what to eat for lunch, but even those seemingly simple choices would require far too much time and energy if not for decision-making heuristics.. Without heuristics, we'd barely be able to make it out the door to start our days.

Salespeople who provide effective short cutting tools experience extremely positive long term results.

Short cut your way to success

Imagine the frustration dog owners experience when they research trainers in the hopes of finding a competent one. Information is often contradictory, misleading, and confusing. The actual methodology used by trainers is frequently obfuscated by weasel speak terminology and that many trainers who claim to be positive reinforcement trainers are not. As clothing retailer Sy Syms once said, "An educated consumer is our best customer." Unfortunately, most dog owners are not highly educated with regard to their four legged friends. Because of this, they tend to rely on short cuts to facilitate the decision making process.

If you want to persuade people, keep your messages short and memorable such as, "We fix dollar haircuts." Be mindful of the fact that for the vast majority of people, free time is scarce and you can best help them to hire you by being mindful of short cut tools such as social proof, perceptual contrast, and the desire to not miss out on something.

6

Mastering the Key Tools: Your Website, Email, and Telephone

You will note that I have not really talked about "marketing" so far in this book. I like to think of marketing as what gets you noticed, sales as what gets you clients. This chapter focuses on the intersection of marketing and sales. Unless someone learns about your training business and contacts you, all of those wonderful sales skills you are learning to master won't do you much good.

A tool called "technology"

In today's world, you need to have a grasp on technology to take advantage of the marketing and sales tools at your disposal. I am a technology nut. I love technology. Every time a new computer, tablet, software program, or an app is introduced, I think, "Ah, this is the one. This will change my life forever. I'll never have to load the dishwasher or iron my clothes again. From now on, life will be all about sipping blue cocktails from a glass with a little umbrella in it while on the beaches of Montego Bay." And like a moth drawn to a light, I'm off and running to the nearest geek store or better still, on-line store, to purchase the latest technologically advanced gizmo.

That said, much as I am madly in love with it, I fully understand that technology is only a tool. Yes, Microsoft Word allows my editor to insert notes in the margins of my manuscript such as, "Does this sentence require a decoder ring in order to be understood?" but Word didn't create the manuscript, I did. As noted astutely by Robert Terson, "It's easier to be a good gardener with the right tools, but it's still *you* who has to do the planting, cultivating and harvesting" (Terson, 2012).

Planting, cultivating, and harvesting—sounds like the sales process.

Many people believe that, because of the internet, salespeople have become as extinct as the horse and buggy. Not true. In the United States alone, one out of every nine workers earns his or her living by trying to get others to make a purchase—a job better known as selling.

Let's take a look at how technology, such as websites, emails, social media, etc. are wonderful tools when utilized to support the sales process, not replace it.

The purpose of your website

The purpose of your website is to build interest, create leads, and motivate the visitor to contact you. Websites that represent professional service companies, such as dog training businesses, are not meant to replace the sales process.

Consider the following statistics about the average time visitors spend on websites. Based on findings by Microsoft Research (Nielsen, 2011), page-visit durations were analyzed for 2,505,873 different web pages that took place during over 10,000 web site visits. Jacob Nielsen noted:

- The average website visit is one minute, with many visitors leaving after 10 to 20 seconds.
- On the average web page visitors read, at most, approximately 20% of the text on the page.

- The first 10 seconds of the page visit are critical for a user's decision to stay or leave. The probability of leaving is very high during these first few seconds for a number of reasons, such as user skepticism based on prior browsing experience.
- If the web page survives the first 10 seconds, users will stay a bit longer. That said, the likelihood of them leaving within the next 20 seconds is extremely high.
- After visitors have stayed on your page for 30 seconds, they continue to leave every second but at a much slower rate than during the first 30 seconds.
- If you can motivate visitors to stay on your page for 30 seconds, there's a decent chance that they'll stay longer, often two minutes or more, which is an eternity on the web.

From Wendy Connick, owner, Tailored Content:

> *A website is not a thinking being, no matter how carefully programmed it is. A website can't and won't consider all of the prospect's needs, because there is no way to program every possible question into it. Odds are that every single prospect will have at least one unusual past experience or future need that the website won't take into consideration. A human salesperson, on the other hand, can come up with different questions for every prospect as needed. A salesperson can also provide a personalized experience that a website just can't match* (Connick, n.d.).

The personal touch is so rare in today's technology driven world that it truly stands out and immediately differentiates you from your competition.

Structuring your website

Other than a debate about what to feed dogs, no topic stimulates more passion than a discussion about whether or not pricing should appear on a trainer's website.

As noted earlier in this book, my goal is to inspire you, not to make you a clone of me. My opinion on this subject is based on my experience as a salesperson. You will find varying perspectives regarding this topic. It is my firm belief that the vast majority of effective, professional salespeople trust that they can do a *much* better job of creating value, building rapport, differentiating their services and persuading their prospective customers than even the best website.

I am fairly convinced that trainers who publish pricing on their website are often motivated by a strong aversion to the sales process, and do so in the hope that their website will sell their services for them. "I'll never do that again—all I got was a million calls asking about my pricing!" This was the reaction from one of my Fetch More Dollars consulting business clients to what transpired when she removed her price list from her website. I have heard this sentiment expressed on several occasions.

Every one of those "million" contacts was a *qualified* potential client. After visiting her website, prospects were sufficiently motivated to initiate contact. Once contact was made, it was simply a matter of communicating enough value to justify pricing and gain a new client.

As noted previously, effective selling is directly linked to the value-creation process—your business is not about your *price*, it's about your *value*. Can you expect your website to do a good job of communicating value? If you are selling office supplies, perhaps, but if you are selling a professional service, websites don't do a good job of creating value.

When selling a product that doesn't require the establishment of a rapport, I generally have no issues with posting pricing on a website. In fact, if you visit my dog training business management software website, dogtrainerconnexion.com, you'll see that I list the product price. I don't need to build a relationship with the prospective customer in order to build value in a software program. For this product, value creation is accomplished through screen captures, videos, and downloads. That said, it's not until I speak directly to prospects that they fully understand the value of the program and what it can do to help build their training business.

On the other hand, if you visit my sales coaching website, fetchmoredollars.com, or my dog training website, risingstardogtraining.com, you won't find a price list on either because both businesses are directly linked to relationship building. In order to maximize the value of my services, I need to first build a rapport with the potential client. Providing pricing prior to building value will result in a potential client who is price focused, rather than value focused. Remember, every price is too high until we build value.

From Andrew Neitlich, Director of The Center for Executive Coaching "If you think of yourself as a trusted advisor, and price based on value, then I would avoid posting your prices on the web site. Also, by posting your hourly rates, you set yourself up as a vendor rather than a relationship-driven advisor" (Neitlich, n.d.).

Another comment I often hear from trainers as justification for including pricing on their websites is, "When I shop online, if I don't see pricing, I immediately move on." Again, a distinction needs to be made between a website that represents a professional services company and one that sells products. I know several people who would run from websites of doctors, veterinarians, attorneys, psychologists and other professionals who posted their pricing. "Root canals, $49.95" or "Overcome your fear of flying, $59.95" are not statements that would motivate me to contact the service provider.

When considering whether or not to list pricing on a website, from my perspective, it's rather simple. If you're selling a professional service, I strongly advise you to not show pricing.

Speaking to prospects through your website

You can build a certain amount of value through your website, but since you are your product, the best way to communicate who you are is by speaking directly with prospective clients. As a rule, people don't visit an online dating site, read a profile, and decide they want to enter into a committed relationship without first speaking with that person. In much the same way, selling our services is about building a relationship. Your prospective client is blitzed with conflicting information while searching the internet for a trainer. Because there are so many unknown factors involved in a purchase decision, the connection that prospect builds with you is a shortcut on which they rely to make their decision. Websites create interest, but if you want to close a sale, open a relationship. The most effective way to accomplish this is by speaking with your prospects. Remember, a solved problem is what the client is paying for. If you aren't able to interact with that client in order to determine what their problem is, how can you justify your pricing?

Often, the reason that a prospective client doesn't purchase a service is because s/he is afraid of making a mistake. You are your prospect's roadmap to success. Think of it this way: If you are driving to a location you've never been before, what makes you feel more comfortable, a full page of written directions that you have to read while navigating the roads, or someone who is very familiar with the route assisting you from the passenger's seat? Your website is the former, while direct contact with the dog owner is the latter. If you steer your clients to make contact with you, you're much more likely to help them make the best purchase decision.

If we embrace that it is our obligation to help the dog owner to hire a great trainer—you—it seems very inconsistent and even a bit uncaring and detached to suggest that a web page can achieve that goal. If we truly want to foster the humane treatment of dogs, we can't do so by avoiding direct contact with prospective clients. If we truly want to help people, the best way to do so is to speak with them.

If you're jittery about not listing your pricing, it may be helpful to explain to your website visitors why you don't do so, and to enlighten them about the next step in the process. Prospective clients might be curious to understand why they need to speak with you first.

The best thing you can do is test it. Remove your pricing from your site for two to four weeks, and compare the results. If you get more inquiries, more sales, and easier conversions, then you know you've hit on a winning solution.

If you remove pricing from your website *and* in fact receive "millions" of calls and you're not prepared to present yourself in a persuasive manner, you will feel as if the removal of pricing from your site wasn't helpful because your success rate won't be high. It's imperative that your discussion with the prospect is persuasive, communicates value and differentiation, and sells you first. If you simply provide pricing without establishing value first, you're essentially doing the same thing as a website that lists pricing—selling with price being your only differentiator. And it's also imperative that you respond quickly to all inquiries.

An additional benefit to speaking directly with potential clients is that you'll gain feedback, which could be extremely valuable. For example, if you are encountering price objections, it would be important to know that. You won't learn this by posting pricing on your website. Those people don't contact you to let you know why they didn't purchase your services. They simply move on to the next website. In fact, you'll have no idea why your business isn't doing as well as it could be—it's all guess work. But by speaking directly to a client, not only can we discover what we could be doing better, we'll also hear about our competitors, what the customer thinks is different about us, what their prior experiences have been, etc.

A client not gained isn't a total loss if you can learn something from the encounter.

And finally, I have consistently experienced that the initial telephone conversation is actually the first training session. In fact, I feel it's the most important training session. During this conversation, I gain information including how to best motivate the owner, lay out the plan, build trust, and motivate the client for the upcoming face-to-face training sessions. When I arrive for that first appointment, a rapport is already established and we hit the ground running. Why? Because of the power of that first phone conversation which cannot be duplicated by a website.

Email: Not the be all and end all

Car for Sale—$16,500.

What do you think of this offering? Are you ready to purchase this vehicle? Are you thinking it's a great value for the price? Of course not. You need more information before you can answer any of those questions.

With that said, how would you respond to a dog owner who sends you this email: "I'm having some issues house training my 10 week old Havanese puppy Zoe. How much do you charge?" Which would you choose from the following four responses:

1. Send an email with multiple attachments about you and your business and quote a price.
2. Write a lengthy response and quote a price.
3. Write a short response and quote a price.
4. Engage the sender and motivate her toward discussing her needs via phone.

If your answer was anything other than #4, sorry—no "click" and liver treat for you.

When you attempt to use e-mail to sell your services to someone who doesn't know you, you can't possibly establish the natural dialog that allows trust to reach a level necessary for the sale to occur. Additionally, you can't create enough value to justify your price, unless your price is extremely low.

The most effective way to close a sale is through a direct phone dialog with the prospective client. When you receive an email requesting pricing information, you'll want to lead the prospect to the phone. Much like the "ET" movie scene in which Elliot uses Reese's Pieces to lure the alien out of hiding, you'll want to do the same. Try to find things within the email, brief as that email may be, to motivate the customer to chat with you via phone. Your chances of making a sale are much greater if you have a chance to speak directly with prospective clients.

Using the email above as an example, I'd respond by complimenting the owner for seeking out professional training. I'd be sure to mention a few positive traits about the breed. I would let her know that I understand her frustration and I would absolutely paint a picture of how great life will be when she no longer has to keep a bottle of Nature's Miracle in her home. I would touch on the fact that her puppy is in a critical growth stage and that I'd be more than willing to set aside some time to discuss how over the next few weeks she could do things to help create the dog she's always wanted. And finally, I would let her know that I wouldn't be doing her a service by simply quoting a price without speaking to her as each owner's needs are unique. I'd also mention that I would only take a few minutes of her time.

> *If you can, stop using e-mail selling altogether...you should think of e-mail as your last resort. If you can learn to pick up the phone without fear, start a trusting conversation... you'll join the thousands of people who have made the breakthrough to the most natural and efficient way of generating sales....* Ari Galper, sales consultant and creator of *Unlock the Game.*

You will absolutely see your rate of converting inquiries into sales rise, dramatically, if you speak to prospective clients on the phone versus simply quoting a price in an email. And as a value added, you can reinforce your behavior with some Reese's Pieces each time you do.

The Bermuda Triangle of emails: the JUNK folder

Here's a quick and easy way to boost your sales: Have you ever had a great discussion with a prospect, followed up with an email, and then never heard from that person again? Listed below are the most common reasons your email could end up in someone's junk folder. Typically, a combination of two or more of these items will cause your email to get junked:

- The sender is not in the recipient's address book.

- The email has an attachment.
- The email has very few characters.
- The email contains words in the subject like "Urgent," "Important" or "Free."
- The subject line is in ALL CAPS.
- The email uses HTML.
- The email contains links.
- The email uses background colors.

When sending an email, always follow up with a quick email to let the recipient know he or she should have received the original and if not, to check the junk folder. If you want to ensure that your original email lands where it should, avoid what's listed above.

The telephone is not an instrument for self-torture

I can't prove this, but my guess is that in the history of mankind, no salesperson has ever died from making a sales related phone call. Getting in and out of your bathtub is actually more dangerous. How's this for a perspective about sales call anxiety? Many dog trainers would rather walk into a home to train an aggressive dog who might bite them than pick up the phone to make a sales call in order to gain that appointment.

Please keep in mind that even the most experienced salespeople (me being one of them) often have issues with making telephone sales calls. Let's face it, picking up the phone and trying to persuade a complete stranger to purchase your services isn't easy mostly because it triggers a fundamental anxiety we all have: fear of rejection.

As I noted earlier, I have made in excess of 13,000 individual sales in the printing industry. And yes, I still have anxiety when picking up the phone. There are a number of effective techniques you can utilize to reduce your anxiety about making sales phone calls.

As the Toastmasters International group says, "You will not get rid of the butterflies, but you can get them flying in formation."

Telephone coping strategies

Here are a few coping strategies you can employ to reduce your phone aversion/anxiety.

- It's enormously important to remember that the phone call you make is not a "cold" call. It's not as if you rented a phone list from the AKC and started calling each owner to sell your training services. Keep in mind, *the prospect contacted you*. They already know they need your services and they *want* you to call back.
- Prepare yourself before making a call. Rehearse your sales presentation until you're completely comfortable with it. Know what your goal is. Most salespeople get themselves into trouble when they simply pick up the phone without having set a goal for the call.
- Create cue cards that list the points you want to communicate, such as differentiation points list that makes you different from other trainers, questions you need to ask, visuals you'd like to communicate, stories you'd like to tell, etc. When I was first working in sales, I brought a notepad to each appointment. Early in the conversation, I'd ask the prospect if it was ok for me to take notes. When I received an affirmative response (I always did) I'd open my notepad to a page where I had written all my cues across the top of the page. I could see them but my prospect couldn't. The comfort level provided by that safety net was invaluable. Your cue cards can provide the same comfort level.
- Visualize a positive outcome. Imagine a great conversation and feeling good afterward. We've all heard the term "self-fulfilling prophesy" originally coined in 1948 by sociologist Robert K. Merton. The definition of a self-fulfilling prophesy states that positive or negative expectations about an outcome influence a person's

behavior and consequently cause those expectations to be fulfilled. Visualize a positive outcome and you'll be amazed at how often reality will match your visualization.

- Try some self-reinforcement by rewarding yourself with something that is meaningful to you after making your calls.
- If you are concerned about interrupting someone when you call, ask "Have I caught you at a good time?"
- If someone rejects your proposal, realize that it could be for any number of reasons that have nothing to do with you. Try not to read too much into the actions of someone else. I once accidentally called a prospect who had already strongly expressed her lack of interest in my product during a prior phone conversation—she went on to become a loyal customer for years.
- Realize that people don't have to answer the phone. If you are calling at a bad time, people often let calls go to voicemail. If they answer the phone, it means they're interested in talking with you.
- Remember that effectively directed anxiety is actually a good thing. When experiencing anxiety our bodies secrete higher levels of adrenaline, which allows us to respond more quickly and efficiently. Moderate anxiety is actually a good thing. Rejection of your proposal isn't personal and shouldn't deter you from striving for success. As Babe Ruth said "Never let the fear of striking out get in your way." Babe Ruth hit 714 home runs and struck out 1,330 times. Or, as Michael Jordan said, "I've missed more than 9,000 shots in my career. I've failed over and over and over again in my life. And that is why I succeed."

Finally, if you get in the habit of giving your dog a treat whenever you make a phone call, your dog will develop a wonderful +CER to you picking up the phone, and don't we all love to make our dogs happy?

So, pick up the phone and make a call—both your dog and your prospect will be happy you did.

Be a telephone rock star

Have you ever attended a rock concert and experienced the energy projected by the band? Do you think the band members could project that same energy if they were seated in chairs for two hours? When speaking on the phone, please stand, walk around, smile a lot, be animated—your energy level will be much higher and you'll sound more alert and engaging.

If you don't believe me, try this experiment. Dial your own number while sitting on a nice comfy couch or chair. Without smiling, leave yourself a phone message. Then, call back and repeat the exercise, only this time, stand up, walk around, be animated, and smile a lot (as the wonderful Victor Borge once said, "The shortest distance between two people is a smile"). Go back and listen to both messages. Who would you be more inclined to call back?

A few words about call backs: If you speak to a prospective client and that conversation ends with the person saying that they need to think things over and they'll be back in touch, you can politely say, "I'm sure you've got other priorities in your life. How about if I call you back on Thursday [or whatever day is two or three days away]?"

And then, do it. If the prospect says that they'd rather call you back, great. Wait a few days and call back anyway.

You'd be amazed at how many people will thank you by saying that they simply got busy and were meaning to call back. You'll also be making a statement about your interest level. If you don't show interest in gaining the customer, exactly what statement does that make to the prospective client about what you're interest level will be after you're hired?

The math is simple: You either avoid calling someone back due to your own discomfort or worry that you'll upset them by doing so, or you make the determination that their dog's quality of life is worth that risk and that s/he and their owners need you.

All math should be so easy.

Sneeze and drop the phone

My first printing customer in 1990 was the Risk and Insurance Management Society (RIMS). I gained them through a cold call, that is, a call that was made without the recipient knowing me or my company.

Before that call, I had not succeeded in my calling efforts. I had worked for hours practicing my phone sales presentation. I even recorded myself in order to review how I sounded. Yet I hadn't been able to convince anyone to schedule an appointment to meet me.

Determined as ever, I dialed company after company on my call list—next up: RIMS. When the print buyer, Ann Lem, answered the phone, I launched into my script. "Hi, my name is John Visconti. I'm calling from…" and I sneezed and dropped the phone. After picking it up, I said "Smooth, huh? I guess I'm allergic to making cold calls."

Amazingly, Ann (who I still keep in touch with today) laughed. What followed was a pleasant, off-script conversation. The important thing to point out is that even though I went off script, due to the countless times I practiced it, I was able to communicate my sales points effortlessly out of sequence from the original scripted version. I realized by simply being myself, by being human rather than stiffly scripted, I had connected with my prospect. Most importantly, I was able to schedule an appointment and eventually gain a customer and a good friend.

Practice makes perfect

Practice your presentation, which means that first, you need to *develop* a presentation.

After you have developed a script to communicate your three or four points of differentiation and the benefits of working with you, rehearse that script until you can recite it backward and forward. You'll want to become so fluent in communicating your key points that you'll be able to seamlessly move in and out of conversations, reciting these points in response to where the conversation takes you, rather than delivering them sequentially in a rigid script.

I am reminded of a story from my childhood which will illustrate the downside of sequentially ordered scripts. My brother accepted a job selling encyclopedias. One night he practiced his memorized script sales presentation on the family. As he made his way through his demo, I noticed that if any of us asked him a question, he'd need to backtrack in order to restart his presentation. Realizing this and of course, being the good sibling that I am, I began to continually ask questions just for the fun of watching him restart his script. I'm fairly certainly that we'd all still be sitting in the living room were it not for the *cut the nonsense* look my dad flashed in my direction.

In fact, you'll want to be so well practiced with your sales presentation that it sounds adlibbed. I have told the same stories hundreds of times and I can pretty much guarantee the first time and the last time I recited them they sounded equally fresh. Doing so will help you build rapport and the experience for your prospect will feel more natural which will lead to a greater connection. No one likes to be sold *to* and that's exactly what a rigid, canned sales script sounds and feels like to a client. If your conversations sounds fresh and follows a natural flow, you'll be much more successful in gaining new clients. You'll also feel less like you're selling and more like you're communicating, connecting, and helping.

This isn't to say that you shouldn't adjust your presentation. Based on results and your growth as a salesperson, it's important to incorporate new elements into your dialog. Doing so will also help to keep you from becoming stale. But it's vitally important to work within a standard framework.

Aside from helping you to gain sales, a well-practiced script provides a safety net that will allow you to feel more comfortable, more at ease, and more likely to be yourself when speaking with prospects.

And remember, if all else fails, you can always sneeze and drop the phone.

What's the appropriate timeframe for responding to a phone inquiry message?

My response to this question is always the same: It depends on how many clients you're willing to lose. Quite honestly, I'm astonished when I'm asked that question or when I hear, "I can't believe I called back the next day and they had already hired another trainer."

Next time you're thinking "I'll call back tomorrow. I have a lot of paperwork to do tonight," I'd like you to picture this: The prospect who left you a phone message just completed a Google search for a dog trainer and is calling each trainer on that list. It would be like spotting a $500 bill on the edge of an overpass on a windy day and thinking "I'll come back tomorrow to pick it up."

Strike while the iron is hot. The early bird catches the worm. He who hesitates is lost. There's no time like the present. Time and tide wait for no one. Call you prospect back immediately or someone else will. It's that simple.

Aside from heading off your competition, keep in mind that prospective clients are never more motivated than when they makes the initial contact. Consequently, your chances for success are never greater.

We live in an instant society. On average it takes people approximately 15 to 20 seconds to become impatient while waiting for an elevator. According to a survey of 2,500 customers from Velaro, a provider of live chat software, 60 percent of participants believe that one minute is too long to be on hold, and

32.3 percent believe that customer service representatives should answer immediately—with no hold time.

Your prospective customer contacted you, which indicates an interest *now*, but it doesn't necessarily guarantee an interest *later*. Call back immediately or you run the risk of the caller losing interest or being sold an inferior training package by another trainer. Call back now or someone else will.

The next time you're tempted to say, "I can't believe I called back the next day and they had already hired another trainer." I'd like you to imagine your response if your FedEx drive exclaimed, "I can't believe you want this package in Columbus, Ohio, by tomorrow!" We live in an instant society. You're probably reading the Kindle version of this book. Call back your prospects as quickly as you can. Doing so is not only good business, it's courteous.

7

The Importance of Being Prepared and Setting Goals

The meeting of preparation with opportunity generates the offspring we call luck.

Anthony Robbins, motivational speaker

Preparation is the only aspect of the sales process over which you have complete control. You can't control anything else about your sales presentation or client interaction; you can *influence and persuade*, but the only time you *control* the process is during preparation. When you prepare, it helps you to add value to the conversation with your prospects. Dog owners who contact you are looking for help. Are you prepared to converse about their goals/problems or, are you simply there to present your offerings much as a peddler would?

Be prepared to fail if you have failed to prepare

Preparation isn't exciting but the results sure are. *Preparing* isn't fun. *Doing* is fun. Planning can feel tedious. But I assure you the results of planning are anything but tedious. Preparation leads to greater self-confidence. Self-confidence leads to greater success.

Preparation will also help to pull you out of a sales slump ditch. Sales slumps are inevitable. All salespeople experience them. A reliable way to end a sales slump is to return to fundamentals. When we "wing it" rather than utilizing a standard presentation, the path back to the fundamentals which are critical for success is a lot more difficult to navigate. When you set your sales GPS, the step by step instructions to your destination are formal. Should you lose your way, you'll be redirected back to your original directions. Without a formal plan, getting back on track is infinitely more difficult.

Often, people don't prepare because they feel they already know the material. Some feel there's simply not enough time to prepare. (Note: If you don't prepare, you'll have plenty of free time as your ability to gain clients is greatly compromised when you're unprepared.) Some people aren't sure how to prepare. And finally some folks simply don't understand the value of being prepared.

Effective salespeople focus most of their time on what they'll be saying *before* they ask for the sale. It's like being a gardener preparing the ground before planting. The most expensive seeds can be planted, but unless the ground has been properly prepped, there's very little chance for the seed to take root.

The same goes for your prospective clients. They deserve to have a prepared, knowledgeable, reliable professional helping them make a very important decision. Before you speak with a prospect, ask yourself, "Would I be impressed by my preparedness?" After you speak with a prospective client, identify which parts of your presentation you can improve upon and get to work on refining them. Your client, and your business, will thank you for it.

Preparing for a sales presentation is no different than preparing for a dog training session. Preparation provides you with the benefits of reducing anxiety, helping you to feel more confident and of course, as a result, an increase in your sales. Since the majority of your competitors don't take the time to prepare, *preparation* is also *differentiation*. When you are prepared, you'll stand out from the crowd of other trainers.

Create a script and list of questions

Create your script, practice, and refine it, and produce a list of generic questions ("What's your dog's name?" "Are there children living in your home?") A "yes" answer to this question opens up several opportunities for you to add value to your sales presentation by introducing the idea of teaching safe interaction between children and dogs. Also create a list of questions specifically for the prospect such as "In your email you noted that your dog guards his food bowl, can you describe his behavior when he does this? How long has your dog been practicing this behavior?" Then create follow-up notes about your business and send them to your prospect after your sales call.

"Ready, fire, aim!" isn't a great strategy when aiming at a target. Prepare and you'll be amazed at how many more bull's eyes you'll score.

Preparing to sell against force-based trainers and whisperers

One of my motivations for writing this book is to help positive reinforcement trainers gain a greater market share and build thriving businesses. But there's also a moral imperative at play here—the humane treatment of dogs. The subject of the potential risks associated with force-based training methods should no longer be up for debate. Countless studies have been conducted, and organizations like the American Veterinary Society of Animal Behavior (AVSAB) have published position papers regarding the use of pain/force/intimidation in training—all of them highlight the immense downsides associated with these methods (AVSAB, n.d.). Since we possess empirical evidence about the risks related to these methods, how do we distill this information into an accessible, memorable message that will motivate our prospective clients to avoid such trainers? What follows are sales presentation points I utilize to demonstrate the benefits of low-risk, positive reinforcement training vs. the pitfalls of high-risk, force-based training.

Returning to my discussion about the importance of emotionally engaging your prospect, it's significant to note that force trainers possess a built-in advantage when it comes to selling their services. Their labels and descriptors such as "dominance," "pack leader," and "alpha" are all highly charged, "sexy" labels that paint visuals and engage emotions. On the other hand, the language of positive reinforcement trainers includes much less charged, scientific terminology like "rate of reinforcement," "extinction burst," and "conditioned emotional response" etc. For most people, science ain't sexy and therefore these terms will do little to motivate them. Because of this, it's vitally important for you to utilize visuals and engage the emotions of your prospective clients through the use of analogies and stories that illustrate clear benefits of force-free training and expose the inherent risks and inefficiencies of force techniques.

Please keep in mind that while it's essential to be informative about your training methodology, advising a prospective client that you are a "force-free" or "positive reinforcement" trainer, while meaningful to you, often doesn't hold the same meaning for the average dog owner. If dogs were making the purchase decision, yes, force-free trainers would win business every time. But, since the decision maker is the dog *owner*, you need to answer their question, "What's in it for me?" Indeed, there are some owners who find force-free methodology intrinsically appealing. These owners will require little or no convincing about your methodology. But for others who have been misled to believe that force trainers don't hurt dogs, that dogs experience pain differently than human beings, that force trainer utilizes a "balanced" approach, or for the owners who are simply unaware of force-free methods (remember Matt OBrien earlier in this book), your approach will need to be different. For these people, it's more important than ever to clearly spell out what *they will gain* by utilizing your methodology versus what *they will lose* by using that of the force-based trainers.

During my sales presentation, I always "back door" my discussion about force vs. positive reinforcement techniques. While I despise heavy-handed training, I never allow my discussion to become a "me vs. them" soap box dissertation being played out on my prospective client's turf. That's not why they contacted me. If you want to partake in a debate about methodology, there are more than enough Facebook groups that will provide you with the opportunity to spend countless hours doing so. Instead, I prefer to interweave my points about the downsides of force training in a proactive manner within the parameters of my sales presentation. By doing so, I have put the force trainers in the position of reacting to me.

I typically start my presentation by noting, "There are only *two ways* to motivate a dog—the avoidance of something unpleasant like pain, fear, and discomfort or the pursuit of something pleasant, like food, toys, and praise. That's it plain and simple, there are only two ways. A warning flag should go up when a trainer hazes the lines between these two approaches or doesn't make clear what approach he/she will utilize. A dog owner who is looking to hire a trainer, at a minimum, has the right to know, specifically, which approach the trainer will use. Clearly, I use the latter—the pursuit of something pleasant. That's not to say that avoidance of pain isn't a powerful motivator. It is. But the downsides associated with this type of training are very high." As a side note, it's very important to avoid stating that force methodology doesn't work. It does. There's a reason positive punishment and negative reinforcement comprise half of Skinner's quadrants of learning. If you state that these approaches don't work, not only are you incorrect, you're also opening the door for a counter response for the dog owner (or competing trainer) to cite instances where in fact, these methods have worked. Instead, the focus should be on the costs, risks, unintended consequences and downsides associated with force methodology.

Once I have established this foundation, I progress to a discussion about *high-risk* vs *low-risk* training. We know there is a huge benefit to low-risk training methodology. But don't assume your prospective clients know this. It's to their advantage that you spell it out for them. I rarely make references to how high-risk methods are often inhumane. This has the potential to be an instant turn-off for some clients because it can come across as very judgmental, particularly if they are considering utilizing them. Remember, during any sales transaction, the client always buys you first so, steer clear of any statements that can be perceived as critical. They'll only serve to create unproductive tension. When persuading my prospect that low-risk and positive reinforcement training is the best option, I always avoid questions such as, "Would you teach your child with heavy-handed methods?" Again, it's potentially confrontational to pose a question like that. And it can also come across as somewhat self-righteous.

Instead, I plainly and objectively note the downsides connected with high-risk, heavy-handed training methods. By doing so, I have immediately categorized force trainers as risky business. I cite how ineffective heavy-handed training techniques are due to the physiological state of high arousal and avoidance behaviors they cause in dogs. I note that the dog is more focused on the avoidance of the aversive punishment than learning and as a result learning, if it occurs at all, often takes much longer to yield positive results. If you recall, one of the challenges encountered during any sales transaction is diminishing fears that the cost of engaging your services (financial as well as the investment of time and effort) will be too high. Informing a client that it will take much longer to achieve positive results and effective behavior modification (rather than behavior suppression) when utilizing force methods magnifies their concerns about the required level of investment. Additionally, using the words "high-risk training" provides a clearly implied negative that, for the benefit of the owner, should be avoided.

During my discussion, I might also point out, "Correction-based, force trainers who apply punishment after the dog performs an unwanted behavior are essentially communicating to the dog, 'Nope. Wrong. Guess again.' It's like a computer that posts a message, "Error type 325 occurred" and provides no additional information before shutting down. Rather than spending innumerable hours chasing after and correcting unwanted behaviors, why not inform the dog of the desired behavior and spend a much shorter amount of time training by reinforcing that behavior?" By framing the process this way, I've sold a benefit to the dog owner—less investment of their time for better results. That's easy math.

As always, my statements are benefits driven and I try to engage the listener emotionally by creating a "verbal video" as Dr. Barbara Sherman, MS, PHD, DVM calls it. "Let's say you are learning to play a musical instrument. How focused would you be on the task at hand if each time you played a sour note, your teacher hit you, shocked you, or caused you some other kind of discomfort? Not only would you not be focused on learning, you'd likely develop a dislike for your teacher. It's no different for dogs. Isn't that something you'd like to avoid?"

Or, how about trying this approach with a prospective client? "Let's say you were learning to hit a baseball? If each time you swung and missed, your coach caused you pain, you would either quit, or perhaps choose to stand perfectly still, aware that if you didn't swing and miss nothing bad could happen. It's important to note, you'd never learn how to hit a baseball using this approach. All you'd learn is how to avoid punishment. The same thing happens with dogs—it's called avoidance behavior and learned helplessness. With force training, dogs learn how to avoid punishment rather than learning what we want to teach them. It may look like the unwanted behavior has disappeared but essentially all the trainer has done is suppress the unwanted behavior, not replace it with a more desired one. For example, when force is utilized in attempting to modify a dog's on leash reactivity to other dogs, just as you'd probably develop a negative association with the sport of baseball in the above example, your dog might develop a negative association with going for walks because they're not a pleasant experience."

With regard to the unintended negative consequences often associated with force training, I recount the following story to illustrate how dogs can associate the pain/discomfort that is delivered by high-risk trainers with something other than what is intended. "When I first brought my dog Pepper home from the shelter, she was very reactive to landscapers running their leaf blowers. One day, upon hearing the sound of a revved up leaf blower, she charged the back door and in doing so, contacted a set of vertical blinds which came crashing down on her. An aversive was delivered (blinds falling) after an undesired behavior (reactivity to the leaf blower) occurred. In the world of force training, this consequence should have served to diminish my dog's reactivity to leaf blowers. But instead, an unintended consequence occurred—she became very fearful of the blinds. Worse yet, she still continued to react every time she heard the leaf blower. And because fear tends to generalize quite easily, it took me weeks to reduce her fear of all the blinds in my home. Force training contains inherent risks. You can never predict how fears acquired while being subjected to force methods might manifest in the future."

In order to head off the accusation that positive reinforcement trainers bribe dogs and are food dependent, I state, "While I am a positive reinforcement trainer, I do not believe in bribing a dog or creating a 'show me the money' dog who will not perform unless food is readily available. We will work toward quickly phasing out food and then only paying for outstanding performance. I don't *reward* dogs, I *pay* them for excellent performance. We will not become food dependent." I sometimes offer the visual of the owner of a shock collar trained dog not being able to walk his dog because the batteries in the remote have died—talk about dependence! Additionally, I note that force trainers have a term called 'collar-savvy' which refers to the dog not responding to cues when the shock, prong, or choke collar isn't around his neck. The dog knows the threat of pain is absent and therefore his reliability with obedience cues goes down the drain. Notice, I never discuss whether or not the use of a shock, prong or choke collar is humane. I focus the discussion on owner benefits and potential risks.

What about whisperers and untrained trainers?

Finally, as a CPDT-KA, I discuss my certification as a way of proactively heading off unschooled "whisperers." Typically, I speak about how the field of dog training is completely unregulated. "The truth is, you could go to Staples tomorrow, purchase some business cards, and call yourself a dog trainer. Hair stylists are required to log 1,000 hours at a board certified school and pass examinations in order to obtain a license to cut your hair. While we all need protection from bad haircuts, I think you'd agree, mishandling a dog has a greater downside yet there are no requirements placed on dog trainers." I find that most owners are very surprised about this information.

I also discuss the requirements one must meet in order to qualify for the certification test. I point out that I must gain CEU's to keep my certification live and that I live by a code of ethics (I inform the prospective client these can be viewed on my training site) as part of my certification. I then point out the difference between trainers being certified by a private school vs. an independent body, such as the CCPDT. I would say something like this: "Let's say you and I decided to open up a school for dog trainers. Our curriculum could be awful. Our teaching skills even worse. At the end of the course, we would test our students and those who passed would receive a diploma. When you hear trainers refer to their certification be sure to ask which independent body has certified them. There's a big difference between passing accounting classes in school vs. being a Certified Public Accountant. Call me wacky but in the future, if I require surgery, I'd like to know my anesthesiologist is board certified."

By incorporating *your* unique strengths, certifications, memberships, etc. into benefits driven, low risk statements, you'll win business from force trainers at a consistent rate.

A goal is a dream scheduled

As we learned from the Harvard Business Review article (Martin, 2011), top salespeople set goals and measure their progress toward those goals just as you set goals for your training appointments. A trainer who "wings it" is much less likely to conduct a productive training session than one who sets goals and measures the dog's and owner's progress toward those goals. It is equally important to set sales goals for your training business. The process of doing so will help to increase your sales in part due to the fact that you have focused on creating goals and measuring progress toward them. Performance which we measure, improves.

As noted by J.C. Penney, "Give me a stock clerk with a goal and I'll give you a man who will make history. Give me a man with no goals and I'll give you a stock clerk."

Setting goals also provides added value by enhancing your present quality of life. Having something to reach for provides a sense of anticipation about the future and, as a result, makes your present life more enjoyable because you're excited about what you're striving to achieve.

Goals also help to determine the kind of person you want to be. At the end of the day, it's less about the goals you achieve, and more about the person you become through striving toward those goals. It's satisfying when you work hard and attain success, but the true prize is often found in the process of achieving those goals.

Of equal importance, establishing realistic goals and a roadmap to achieve them will help you grow your business, gain more clients, and help more dogs.

Set your goals and then set sail

In your dog training business, you are your own sales manager, and all good sales managers set goals for their staff. Yes, you've just earned a promotion to sales manager. This book is already paying off a return on your investment with your first promotion. Congratulations.

Below are some steps that will help you to create your formal goals and "things to do" list.

Step 1. Define your objectives and make them quantifiable. How many new customers would you like to add per month? What would you like your sales to be for the next month, quarter, or year? When will you have your formal sales presentation completed, including your points of differentiation, list of questions, benefits, and value? When setting goals, it's important to be as specific as possible. "I'd like to acquire more clients" is not a productive way to express a goal. A goal needs to be measurable in order to be worth striving for.

Writing down your goals can be a very effective way to help to make them become a reality. A study by Dave Kohl, professor emeritus at Virginia Tech, found that people who regularly commit their goals to writing earn nine times as much over their lifetimes as those who don't. Another study that was performed by Dr. Gail Matthews, of the Dominican University of California, confirmed that writing down your goals results in a greater success rate (Duke Chronicle, 2011 and Dominican News, n.d.).

By simply committing your goals to writing, you are subconsciously setting them into motion. You're instructing your brain to focus on them, and strive toward achieving them. Goal-oriented people often go to much greater measures to ensure they hit their goals when they write them down.

When you write your goals down, try not to keep them a secret. Share your goals with at least one friend. Years ago, my good friend Kevin decided he wanted to try skydiving. He set up an appointment to do so and then informed me about his plan. He didn't tell a bunch of people (out of concern that if he backed out, he'd hear a lot of ribbing), but figured if he told at least one person, he'd be more likely to take the plunge, so to speak. I'm happy to report that Kevin saw his plan through and lived to tell about it.

Step 2. Create a plan to succeed by breaking your goals down into steps. Let's say your goal is to add 20 new clients in the next two months. Your milestone goals might look like this:

- Deliver promotional material to 15 veterinarians.
- Conduct a lecture at a library, community outreach program, or school.
- Deliver information about your business to three local shelters.
- Distribute promotional brochures to four local dog food stores.

Step 3. Execute your plan. Take action.

Step 4. Reinforce your positive behavior to stay motivated. List the five most important things you need to do the next day to move your goal further ahead. The most successful sales people understand that daily discipline is the key to the achievement of goals. Then find a way to reward yourself after your daily goals are met. Along with your written daily "things to do" list, include a note about what the payoff will be for completing the items on your list.

The difference between top sales performers and the rest of the field is clear. Top performers have a plan to achieve their goals, and they act on that plan every day. Design a daily and/or weekly plan, act on it consistently, monitor your results, learn as you progress, and make adjustments as necessary.

As Zig Ziglar noted, the best salespeople are "experienced rookies." By that he means they view the selling process as a continuing education. Routine review of your goals should be part of your goal-setting process. As dog trainers, we are committed to ongoing education about our field. The discipline of sales is no different.

Be prepared for occasional bumps in the road. In fact, try to welcome them, as we typically learn more from what goes wrong than what goes right. Ask yourself, "Have I failed recently?" and if the answer is "no" it means you're playing too close to the vest. I am reminded of the Hall of Fame coach Bill Parcells stating to his quarterback, Phil Simms, "Simms if you don't throw two interceptions [throwing the ball into the hands of the opposing team] today, you ain't trying." Parcells wanted to help Simms overcome fear of failure which was limiting his ability to reach his full potential as a quarterback. Phil Simms went on to guide his team to a Super Bowl win with a record setting performance in 1987.

Of course, success feels better than failure. But in the end, any meaningful success likely will have arisen out of failures during your journey. Having the confidence to succeed requires having the courage to fail. That said, the only true failures are the ones we don't learn from. In the words of Thomas Edison, "I have not failed. I've just found 10,000 ways that won't work. Many of life's failures are people who did not realize how close they were to success when they gave up."

Set your goals, and then set sail with one hand on the rudder. Once you do, you'll be delighted with your journey and the arrival at your destination.

To flea or not to flea that is the question

Fleas are known for their ability to jump. In order to limit them from doing so, flea trainers place them in a jar and then screw the lid on. After jumping and continually banging their heads on the lid, the fleas learn to limit themselves, to jump just high enough to avoid hitting the lid (aka, passive training).

The trainer removes the lid and the fleas will self-limit and not jump any higher than where the lid used to be. The fleas can now be kept in the jar, without a lid on it. I guess you could say the fleas have learned a lesson in the school of hard knocks.

My hope for you is that you won't limit yourself like a flea—fleas aren't good for dogs. It is my strongest desire that you'll utilize the unique skill set you already possess and that you'll believe in yourself and the tremendous good you do for others in order to fetch more clients and help more dogs—they deserve it and so do you.

About the Author

John D. Visconti, CPDT-KA is the owner of Rising Star Dog Training Services, LLC; Rising Star Dog Training, LLC; Dog Trainer ConneXion business management software; and Fetch More Dollars sales consulting. He has written several columns for the *APDT Chronicle of the Dog* magazine and is a regular columnist for the PPG newsletter, *Barks from the Guild.* He has also served as a chair for the APDT Business Subcommittee. John has presented several sales coaching lectures and webinars to dog training schools and force-free organizations. Additionally, during 23 years in corporate life, John has been a sales consultant, sales manager and salesperson. He is also an award winning and published songwriter and performer.

After an unfulfilled lifelong pursuit of his dream to run the machine that inserts the cream into Hostess Twinkies, he turned his attention to a secondary dream and wrote this book. In a synergistic blend of both dreams, he will consider sending a free package of Twinkies to anyone who is disappointed with their purchase of this book.

References

AVSAB position statements are available here: http://avsabonline.org/resources/position-statements.

Christy, Theresa. Otis Elevator Co.

Cialdini, Robert B. *Influence: Science and Practice*, Pearson, Kindle Ebook (5th Edition), 2009, Kindle location 5311.

Connick, Wendy. http://sales.about.com/od/salesbasics/a/Selling-Better-Than-Your-Website.htm

Dooley, Roger. *Brainfluence: 100 Ways to Persuade and Convince Consumers with Neuromarketing*. Page 7, loc 707

Goldstein, Noah; Martin, Steve; and Cialdini, Robert. *Yes! 50 Scientifically Proven Ways to be Persuasive*, Simon and Schuster, 2008

Grant, A. "Rethinking the Extraverted Sales Ideal: The Ambivert Advantage." *Association for Psychological Science*, 24(6), (2013); 1024–1030.

Dominican.edu/dominicannews/study-backs-up-strategies-for-achieving-goals

Dukechronicle.com/articles/2011/04/06/reflections-compulsive-goal-setter

Martin, Steven. "Seven Personality Traits of Top Salespeople." *Harvard Business Review*, June 2011 (retrieved from http://blogs.hbr.org/2011/06/the-seven-personality-traits-o/ April 2014).

Monarch Telecom. http://www.monarchti.com/how-long-will-you-wait-on-hold/

Neitlich, Andrew. http://www.sitepoint.com/should-you-post-prices-on-your-website/

Nielsen, Jakob. "How Long Do Users Stay on Web Pages?" *Nielsen Norman Group*, June 12, 2011 (retrieved from www.nngroup.com/articles/how-long-do-users-stay-on-web-pages/ April 2014).

NPR.org/blogs/health/2012/11/26/165570502/give-and-take-how-the-rule-of-reciprocation-binds-us

Pink, Daniel H. *To Sell Is Human: The Surprising Truth About Moving Others*. Riverhead, reprint edition, 2012, Page 19.

Pozin, Ilya. "9 Biggest Mistakes Entrepreneurs Make." *Time Business and Money*, July 2013 (retrieved from http://business.time.com/2013/07/11/9-biggest-mistakes-new-entrepreneurs-make/ April 2014).

Searchenginejournal.com/the-power-of-social%C2%A0proof/21896/

Simmons, Annette. *Whoever Tells the Best Story Wins: How to Use Your Own Stories to Communicate with Power and Impact*. AMACOM, 1st edition, 2007.

Terson, Robert. *Selling Fearlessly: A Master Saleman's Secrets for the One-Call-Close Salesperson*. Winthrop and Foster Publishing, 2012.

Richard van Houten, Bron and Partners. http://www.bronpartners.nl/documents/sentence.pdf

Ziglar, Zig. *Ziglar on Selling: The Ultimate Handbook for the Complete Sales Professional*, 2007.

Index

Also available from Dogwise Publishing

Go to www.dogwise.com for more books and ebooks.

How to Run a Dog Business

Putting Your Career Where Your Heart Is, 2nd Ed.

Veronica Boutelle

This second edition, incorporating Veronica's ten years of experience helping dog pros succeed, included additional advice on packaging services, setting policies, and avoiding burnout, an expanded marketing chapter and resources section, and two entirely new chapters covering online marketing and developing the perfect staff.

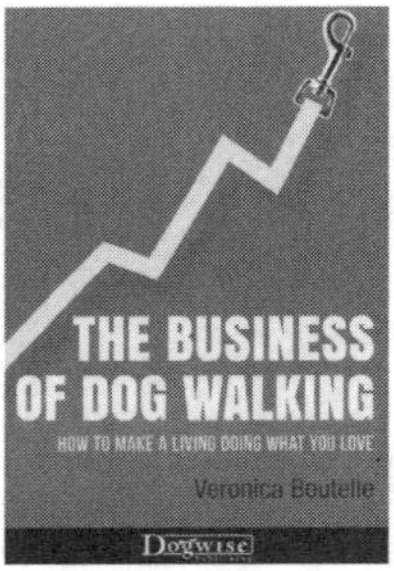

The Business of Dog Walking

How to Make a Living Doing What You Love

Veronica Boutelle

Professional dog walking is a booming business. *The Business of Dog Walking* is a comprehensive guide to creating—or improving—a solid dog-walking business. To be a successful dog walker, you must be dog savvy and business savvy, a combination of skills that do not always come natural to people. If you are serious about becoming a professional dog walker, this book is a must-read.

On Talking Terms with Dogs

Calming Signals, 2nd Ed.

Turid Rugaas

Norwegian dog trainer and behaviorist Turid Rugaas is a noted expert on canine body language, notably "calming signals," which are signals dogs use to avoid conflict, invite play, and communicate a wide range of information to other dogs and people. These are the dogs' attempt to defuse situations that otherwise might result in fights or aggression.

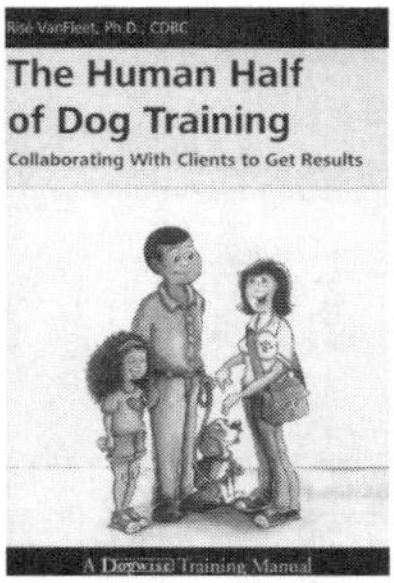

The Human Half of Dog Training

Subtitle

Risë VanFleet

One challenge for many trainers is that their success with dogs ultimately depends on the cooperation, understanding and follow-through of the people whose dogs are being trained. In *The Human Half of Dog Training*, author Risë VanFleet draws upon her experience as a child and family psychologist to teach dog trainers how to take a collaborative approach with clients to help insure the best possible outcomes for their dogs.